Short Essays on Influential
Thinkers and Designers
in Architecture

David Erdman

INTRODUCING

Published by Applied Research and Design Publishing, an imprint of ORO Editions.
Gordon Goff: Publisher

www.appliedresearchanddesign.com
info@appliedresearchanddesign.com

Author: David Erdman
Editor: Original Copy
Book Design: Kammy Leung, Joonmo Ai / Original Copy
Project Manager: Jake Anderson

10 9 8 7 6 5 4 3 2 1 First Edition

ISBN: 978-1-940743-55-4

Color Separations and Printing: ORO Group Ltd.
Printed in China.

AR+D Publishing makes a continuous effort to minimize the overall carbon footprint of its publications. As
part of this goal, AR+D, in association with Global ReLeaf, arranges to plant trees to replace those used
in the manufacturing of the paper produced for its books. Global ReLeaf is an international campaign run
by American Forests, one of the world's oldest nonprofit conservation organizations. Global ReLeaf is
American Forests' education and action program that helps individuals, organizations, agencies, and
corporations improve the local and global environment by planting and caring for trees.

TABLE OF CONTENTS

FOREWORD
INTRODUCING

BY
COLE ROSKAM

Associate professor of architectural history and theory
Department of Architecture at the University of Hong Kong

I read David Erdman's introductions as the discursive equivalent of depth finders. Not depth charges, mind you—those fuse-packed cylinders used to destroy submarines through hydraulic shock. But depth finders—instruments designed to discern and measure unseen distances and volumes.

The texts collected in this book were originally delivered as part of the public lecture series Erdman organized in the Department of Architecture at the University of Hong Kong between 2012 and 2013. In eschewing a more formulaic recital of a speaker's credentials—such as publications, institutions, and projects—Erdman seized an opportunity to collect and curate the ideas circulating through a speaker's curriculum vitae,

Lecture series posters on display after receiving a design award at HKDC 2012.

our department, and the discipline at a particular point in time, reframing them into instructive points of departure. The terms sounded familiar—scale, form, materiality, project, place, etc. But their discursive implications seemed different and somehow more consequential. In front of a diverse and international faculty and student body, Erdman's speculative reworking of these words and their meanings felt both provocative and necessary.

These texts, refined and reassembled here, take on additional meaning in relation to the ways in which the writing of architecture—criticism, theory, and history—continues to adapt to the effects of today's consume-first-process-later digital smorgasbord. Erdman is not the first to absorb the changes afoot; in 2012, for example, renowned architecture critic Paul Goldberger lectured on these shifts and the role of "Architectural Criticism in the Age of Twitter" in accepting the Vincent Scully Prize at the National Building Museum. Goldberger argued for criticism's enduring agency in shaping both ideas and built environments, even as he cast a wary eye toward digital media platforms like Instagram, Snapchat, WeChat, Tik Tok, and Twitter—the image-saturated landscape they support—and their implications for architectural meaning.

Erdman's texts implicitly respond to the same thorny questions posed by new media in relationship to the design of discourse. Social media can bring out the worst in people, but what it brings out in architecture, in particular how we talk and write about buildings, very much remains a work in progress. Early results may gesture toward a total eclipse of the text amid a staccato flurry of image-making gone wild, though as Erdman's punchy preambles suggest, there is still plenty of time and room for new methods of engagement that can test the depth and quality of an argument without unduly testing our attention spans. The material presented here acknowledges the channels through which we currently digest and circulate information without acquiescing to them.

That's not to say more nimble and reflexive forms of discourse don't require old-fashioned hard work. Saying more with less is hard. I shared an office wall with Erdman and could hear him rehearse and hone in on a particular term or topic that would subsequently emerge as a key concept for further discussion either during the lecture and the Q&A, or over the faculty's dinner with the guest speaker. Over the six years that I worked with Erdman, I watched as the positions articulated here took shape through all kinds of media and in many different environments, including conversations at work, notes in class, debate over drinks, photographs and texts circulated on study trips, and now on these pages as a book.

Like any talented designer, Erdman has identified a space and opportunity for experimentation, and transformed it into something new. Just as architecture is itself an anticipatory discipline, so do these texts anticipate what might come next. This may yet kill that, but it may not.

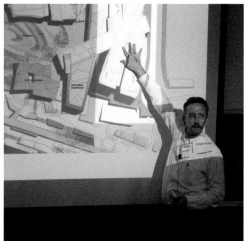

INTRODUCING
INTRODUCING

BY
DAVID ERDMAN

The days of extended architectural essays—labored over, meticulously crafted, and strewn out via a limited set of printed journals—effectively ended at the turn of the century; one could argue that it was even a decade or so before. Some praised while others lamented the end of critical theory and the rise of the post-critical; the end of the digital turn and the rise of the post-digital. Certainly, no matter where one falls within these provocative turns, shifts, and proclamations, something has changed. Those print journals no longer exist. Content about the discipline is instead delivered in compressed snippets in e-zines and blogs, and in the post-text era of Instagram we communicate first and foremost visually. Questions

HKU lecture poster, On_Speed, Spring 2012

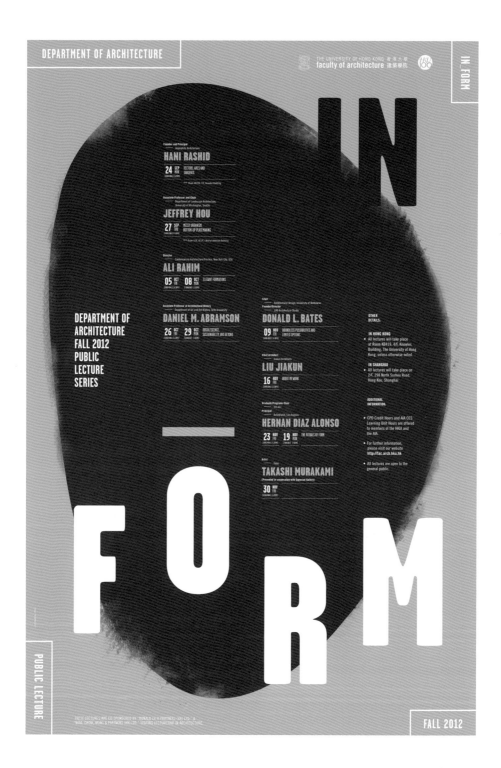

INTRODUCING

about how we sustain productive, theoretical discourse surrounding architectural work, projects, and the ideas behind them are increasingly pressing. Does architectural discourse have the resilience to deal with the speed of new media, and if it does, in what form might that discourse be delivered?

This book did not start as a book, nor a writing project. It is oratory in its underpinnings and was almost accidental in its formation. In 2011, I was given the task of assembling the lecture series while teaching at the University of Hong Kong. It became increasingly clear that the "Lecture Series" format in and of itself was ripe with potential as a platform for engaging students and the broader design and professional communities of Hong Kong. The "Lecture Series," (broadly speaking) is typically not curated. They are a somewhat random selection of thinkers and designers with personal or geographical connections to an institution.

At the turn of the century such series were becoming stale, almost marketing ploys for renowned architects to advertise their work or for emerging architects to pontificate their oblique manifestos. Symposia were where one might find meaningful thematic content, though expounded over hours and days and regularly compiled into lengthy survey books on those themes; often documents more for the participants and institutions than they might be for students or extra-disciplinary audiences.

What occurred to me was the potential to use the lecture series as a platform to introduce ideas—to truly curate each grouping of lectures as a series, and shape the reading and understanding of the lectures in ways that may be entirely oblique to the presenter's intentions yet useful to the students and curricular issues we were trying to articulate as a faculty at HKU. The introduction of each speaker became the setup, an instrument to inflect and launch the lecture and ensuing discussion. To explore this idea, I gave each semester-long series a broad and provocative theme, and attempted to gather voices who would bring together contradictory and parallel perspectives surrounding that theme.

HKU lecture poster, In_Form, Fall 2012

I spent considerable time constructing a 500–1,000-word, 10- to 15-minute introduction to each speaker. The lectures were presented in the typical 45-minute to one-hour format, while the series collecting the broader themes unfolded over the course of a semester, with days or weeks spanning between lectures and the participants never meeting nor speaking together. The introductions took on the key role of producing a continuity of ideas and discourse across the participants and multi-week time frame.

To be clear, the strategy laid out above is a post facto accounting of the formulation of this project. In real time, it unfolded somewhat organically and unknowingly. Presenters often awkwardly indicated that the introduction eclipsed their presentations; faculty and peers simultaneously encouraged me to collect the introductions for publication as much as they asked me to refrain from them; and for students, the introductions were as crucial as they were an annoyance.

I felt a degree of discomfort in the act of introducing, whether the speaker was a friend, colleague, or new acquaintance. It was with this sense of unease that I realized that the introduction itself (be it for a lecture or monograph) had been overlooked and under-tapped as a medium and platform for architecture discourse. Often the things that are the least comfortable are the most productive. Furthermore, as I became more aware of the introduction's role in each lecture, I began to more regularly ponder how it might be a contemporary counterpoint to the long essay and a viable vehicle for discourse in today's Twitter, Instagram, and e-zine climate.

Introducing documents 18 introductions, in the order they were delivered between 2012 and 2013 at Hong Kong University, within the framework of each themed and curated lecture series: On_Speed, In_Form and Project_ing. Each term is verb-like, active, duplicitous, and with a broad enough meaning to include both anticipated and unanticipated participants, readings, understandings, and formations in contemporary discourse.

HKU lecture poster, Project_ing, Spring 2013

■ INTRODUCING

Each introduction is generated from a written text. Originally these were not written for publication but for delivery on stage, developed as a screenplay of sorts. Over time I developed a "template" with a similar structure and flow of information for each essay, allowing for a repetitiousness of method and format while also allowing for the flexibility and necessary room to articulate the different characteristics of each participant (see diagram on pages 18-19). Each introduction is published for the most part as originally written (with the exception of the introductions of Wolf D. Prix, Toyo Ito, and Jesse Reiser, which were written after the event, due to my absence), with the length and basic structure intact. Of course, editing was necessary to clarify points and insure that (in printed format) the introductions are similarly if not more precisely impactful.

The book owes its format to other related book projects or series that charted a course for this type of introductory thinking. While certainly Eric Owen Moss's *Who Says What Architecture Is* (originally published in 2007 and republished as *Coughing Up The Moon* in 2015) predates this book and has similarities in that both collect introductions, the precedents that underpin this project are not limited to this single book, which I would suggest has a different ontological and projective set of intentions. Instead, I would cite the triangulated space between Joan Ockman's *Architecture Culture 1943-1968: A Documentary Anthology* (1993), Albert Pope's *Ladders* (1996), and more recently, Sarah Whiting's *POINT: Essays on Architecture* series (2011-present), each of which makes abundantly evident the increasing condensation of discourse over time; importantly without a correlated dilution of meaning or value.

The flurry of surveys and collections exfoliating from major publishing houses and the absence, if not entire elimination, of funded monographs in the realm of architecture theory and discourse, points also to the lack of audience for the long essay and the simultaneous dilution of content that invokes the all-too-obvious anxieties about our discourse and its impacts (or lack thereof).

These architectural precursors and prior cases are underscored by similar trends in other disciplines, notably art history with its parallel proliferation of

14

short form books on artists from publishers like Taschen and Phaidon, among others, which similarly point to the loss or omission of "serious" theoretical writings on art history and a requisite disciplinary anxiety about their vehicle for discourse.

Perhaps the most pertinent examples underscoring the origins of this book come from literature and specifically from books like Thomas Pynchon's *Slow Learner* (1984). A collection of early career, short-form essays reinforces the general opinion by literary critics (and the author alike) that his most impactful contribution to literature may have been his 150-page *The Crying of Lot 49* (1966), and not *Gravity's Rainbow* or any other of his epic tomes. The book spells out that these earlier projects may have had the seeds of later, longer works and may have been even more meaningful. Related are David Foster Wallace's collected essays on tennis, *String Theory* (2016), which compiles articles for various journals that concisely and in short form expound upon innovative observations in tennis that sports experts could not elucidate. Important here is that Foster Wallace is known in literary circles largely for *Infinite Jest* (1996), a 1,079-page, highly decorated book. Personally, however, I regard the essays in *String Theory* or, for example, his commencement speech-turned-book *This is Water* (2009) as a signal of his capacity to deliver equally impactful work in short snippets that broaden a series of close readings that unpack the technical prowess of tennis players (or the human condition) to an non-literary audience.

All of this is to point out that for today's discourse to propagate and for the younger generation engaging that culture, it may be more appropriate to understand architecture discourse formation as an ensemble of "singles"— meaning 45 records or single MP4s—as opposed to a-priori formations of epic, orchestrated albums like The Beatles' *Sgt. Peppers*, The Who's *Quadrophenia*, or any other generational examples we might point to that align with the historical advance of the long essay in architecture culture.

The overall intent is, therefore, to go deep, fast. The attempt is to cut to the chase and elucidate why these architects and thinkers are important to discourse and the profession; from my understanding of their work and from my personal perspective. By swiftly delivering to the audience benchmarks, handles, and valves that allow you to formulate your own trajectory and discourse surrounding the work, my hope is that this format of short writing introductions is a valuable and useful contribution to our collective interest in design thinking and architecture and our commitment to maintaining its role as a beacon for thought leadership.

POWER OF PLACE

INTRODUCING
KENGO KUMA

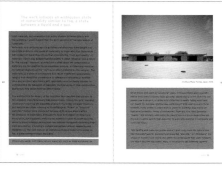

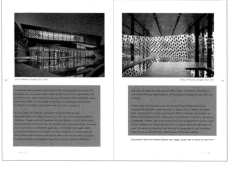

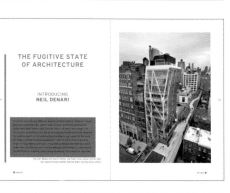

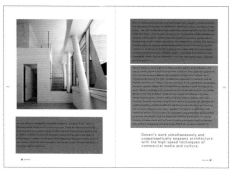

THE FUGITIVE STATE
OF ARCHITECTURE

INTRODUCING
NEIL DENARI

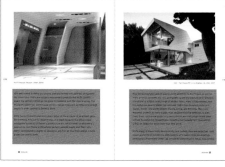

THE ARTLESS DRAWING
Neil Denari, 1962-1998

UNTITLED

INTRODUCING
TAKASHI MURAKAMI

From an architectural perspective, Murakami's work suggests a form of prototyping and iterative development that allows each different medium and iteration to become its own "project".

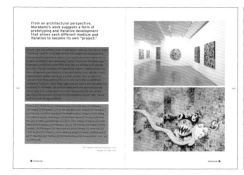

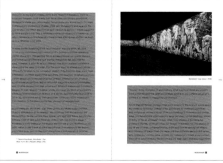

Murakami uses the contrast between what is on the surface and what is behind it as means to engage our perceptions.

PROVOCATION

DISCOURSE BEACON

THE POINT

ON_SPEED

Architecture is in a state of extreme acceleration. Not only have mass production and computer technology increased the frequency of the production of architecture, but the last 15 to 20 years have also seen an acceleration of architecture discourse, its disposition to critical theory, and new methods of theorizing work through production. Speed has been an equally dominating force collapsing the space between the urban and exurban; between the national and international; densifying and mixing the populations, the economic structures, the social structures, and the geopolitics that situate/resituate architecture discourse and the contexts of the built environment.

Speed comes with controversy. There is increased concern about the inequities, displacements, and relative injustice that is understood to be an outcome of speed—blurring and overlooking the individual in favor of economic or political gain. Nonetheless, it is precisely these mechanisms and this speed that afford a conceptual, economic, and social space within which mainstream architecture operates. It is a fact that urban development is directly linked to transport and supply chains underpinning the rate of construction and volume of finance necessary for building cities.

Speed is (if nothing else) an unstable and bi-directional concept worth examining and affronting, because of its inextricable presence in our cities, buildings, and disciplinary culture. This line of inquiry, between the propulsive and convulsive affects of speed, forms this chapter, opening up a discussion which is as much an examination of the architectural discourse of speed and cities, as it is about buildings that mediate on the accelerative effects and aesthetics of speed.

Speed is one way we can precisely discuss the design attributes of architecture within the city in tandem with architecture's urban vicissitudes. Where acceleration is predominately focused on rates over time, speed introduces the notion of distance and location; marrying the pace and cadence of architectural experience with its contextual dimensions, distances, and locales.

Speed as a subject is firmly lodged in early to mid-20th-century modernist discourse where it asserted its importance as a bridge between the architectural and the urban; take as a case in point Villa Savoye, which uses its port cochère, ramp, and "strip" windows as architectural mechanisms to both accelerate rates and experiences of "the domicile," as well as to dislocate/reconnect the city and the villa—expanding and collapsing distance and proximities of urban and exurban territories. Speed thus serves as an important and operative term that persists in contemporary discourse and practice today, and which must straddle a multitude of scales of work in order to engage the city and its exurban counterparts.

The following introductions bring together differing practices of architecture and varied perspectives of the discourse on speed, which augment and perhaps contradict our presumptive associations of that discourse. The work alluded to spans the gamut from the social politics of place, materialism, and the hand-drawn to the groundless speeds of

exurban and urban megalopoles;
all of which actively engage some
aspect of speed. The framework for
collecting this particular group of
designers, architects, and thinkers
is to inflect their work and give it a
new reading; one that they likely have
yet to consider themselves but which
is evident in the latent possibilities
of their work and pertinent to a
21st-century understanding of how
speed continues to be a useful hinge
between architectural design, its
flows, its ethics, its economies, and
the experiences and cultures of the
contemporary city.

DESIGN: INTELLIGENCE vs. IDEOLOGY

INTRODUCING
MICHAEL SPEAKS

Recently, it has been suggested that critical theory is dead. For someone like Michael Speaks, who is largely known for his curatorial projects and influential writings on architecture, this presumed fact could be detrimental, especially if you believe that criticality is that which is slow, thoughtful, and responsible and that which is not critical is fast, thoughtless, and irresponsible. With exhibitions like *Big Soft Orange* (1998-2000), which introduced the innovation of contemporary Dutch architecture to the world, and articles with titles like "Framing at the Speed of Urban Life" (2011), "Prototyping the Future of Design Research" (2010), and "Intelligence After Theory" (2007) one might get the hint that Speaks does not operate at the conventional, long form "speeds" of

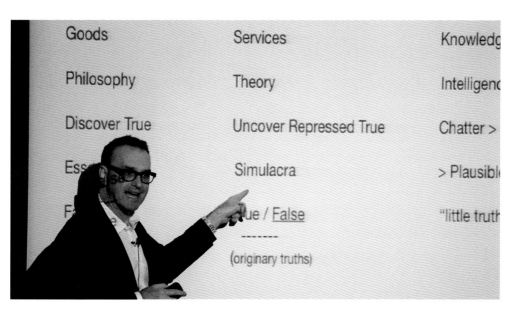

Goods	Services	Knowledg
Philosophy	Theory	Intelligen
Discover True	Uncover Repressed True	Chatter >
Ess	Simulacra	> Plausibl
F	ue / False	"little truth

	(originary truths)	

Michael Speaks at HKU in Spring 2012

critical discourse. In fact, the original title for his lecture was "Architecture at the Speed of Thought"—and unbeknown to him it was the seed of how I came up with this lecture theme, On_Speed.

His resistance to stabilize categories between theory, practice, pragmatics, and intelligence is a turbulent and complex arena in which to negotiate our discourse. It may make us uncomfortable to suggest that one can "prototype research." Speaks's discourse stands out among others for its unique position between the poles of critical theory and practice. It is a discourse borne out of his work with Frederic Jameson, who was a master at pairing corporate architecture with his textual anchor of postmodern architectural theory using none other than the corporate architect John Portman and his Westin Bonaventure Hotel as his instrument and hammer.

Speaks is one of the only writers and thinkers who makes regular studio visits to your office and who really wants to understand both your process and to discuss how that work relates to the discourse, to the economy, and to the

He has taken on the difficult project of redefining "design intelligence," eviscerating it of its biblical underpinnings, and launching it in architecture discourse as a term that binds the quick modes of mass production and modeling with intellectual thought and innovation.

political spectrum. He has taken on the difficult project of redefining "design intelligence," eviscerating it of its biblical underpinnings, and launching it in architecture discourse as a term that binds the quick modes of mass production and modeling with intellectual thought and innovation.

Speaks has written and edited a constellation of significant journals, books, and articles, and he has taught at numerous schools. His ability to move between contentious areas of architecture discourse is paired with his ability to move between disciplines like architecture, art, and graphic design; or between geographical discourses such as the Netherlands, Japan, and the United States.

As a dean, he has heightened the importance of architectural thinking not only within the university but also within the broader sociopolitical milieu surrounding architecture. He has participated as a juror in international competitions like the Taipei Pop Music Center, and has sat on design review boards and government task forces. These are extra-disciplinary venues that reflect a deep commitment to thinking about design as a form of intelligence unique to architecture and necessary for innovation. Perhaps this intelligence, mobility, and speed are more valuable than the "design itself" and allow one to skirt ideology, thus situating the namesake of the lecture tonight between these two poles—intelligence vs. ideology. Please welcome Michael Speaks.

Big Soft Orange exhibition newsprint, Storefront for Art and Architecture, New York, NY, USA, 1999

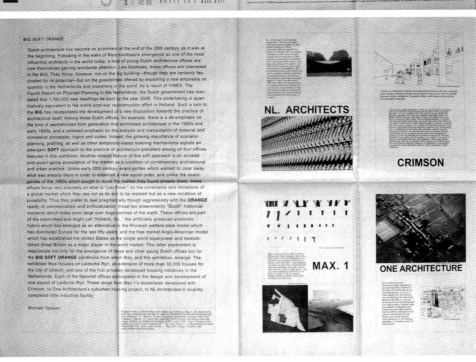

INTRODUCING
PAUL LEWIS

Of the many oppositions we struggle with in the discipline of architecture, none is perhaps more present than the distinction between drawing and building. As Alberti noted, drawing is what separates "Architecture" from "building." Rarely do practices mired in representational theory and drawing bear fruit in the world of building. These are often the theoretical architects we might presume to be too radical or thoughtful for anyone to execute their work—it would take too long or it is too difficult. There is an implicit slowness to drawing, heightened further when you compare

Top: perspectival sectional, New Taipei City Museum of Art, 2011
Bottom: 3H lead drawing on 4mm mylar, Park Tower, 2004

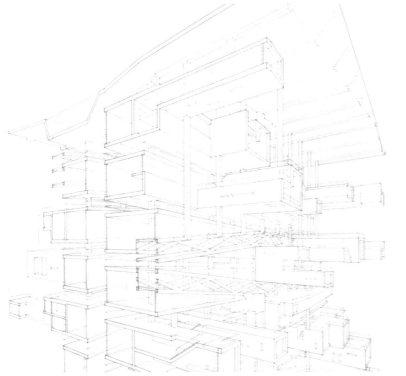

Dash Dogs, New York, NY, USA, 2005

hand drawing to computer drawing or when you compare traditional building
fabrication to digital fabrication. This is the dichotomy between what is a fast,
virtual, and increasingly generic world of AutoCAD and digital fabrication and
a slow, crafted, and quirky world of the hand-made and hand-drawn.

Paul Lewis and his practice Lewis.Tsurumaki.Lewis (LTL Architects) have
located their work directly between these territories of our discipline. Their
drawings are amongst the most compelling coming out of any contemporary
firm. Predominately perspectival sections, the drawings appear hand-drawn
but are a hybrid of the hand and the computer; they appear three-dimensional
but play on two dimensions. Their work uncomfortably rests somewhere
between the meticulously crafted and computationally produced, between the
representation of architecture and its artifact.

Their work uncomfortably rests somewhere between the meticulously crafted and computationally produced, between the representation of architecture and its artifact.

LTL serves as an interesting breed of practice; they are immersed in design research and teaching, while actively building. It is a practice that will design and build a small neighborhood bakery and design large projects for universities like Cornell and NYU, a contemporary art museum, or a buffet in Las Vegas for MGM. As they refer to it in their book *Opportunistic Architecture* (2008), this "promiscuity" is one component of the "opportunism" that defines their practice.

Representation and building are enmeshed in LTL's work. Some of their work has the direct trace of drawings built into them. Dividing lines manifest as counter tops, vertical and horizontal planar cuts manifest as datums, terminating along sharp planes that slice and virtually divide space.

Their obsession with drawing and "the section" is evident in projects they have done for various installations, including names like "Cut: Revealing the Section" or projects named "Dash," where the hidden subtext of dashed lines becomes a spatio-graphic device built into the space.

Even though it is computationally driven and rationalized, the hand is evident in all of their work. Part of this is due to the esoteric fabrication techniques that are taken on board within their practice. Drawings become full scale scripts for installation instructions, where simple prefabricated elements like bamboo skewers are installed into ceilings to become a delirious shaggy swirl of texture overhead—as LTL puts it, "getting less to do more." Many experiments installed in venues like MoMA, SFMOMA, the Cooper Hewitt, and the Architectural League have been leveraged into built work.

33

34

The work combines the simplicity of material and construction with unique and complex patterns of installation —only afforded through their intense understanding of drawing.

At LTL design research is not separate from their practice. They have not only completed numerous installations but have also undertaken a variety of research projects with MoMA and New York City, looking at new hybrids of park, parking, and tower or how to deal with the inevitability of rising water levels. Each examination is paired with a unique set of representations that fall somewhere between the hand and the computer, the literally drawn and the virtually built.

A Rome Prize fellow, assistant professor at Princeton University for over 10 years, and a visiting professor at Columbia and Cooper Union, Lewis traverses the rather intense and difficult terrain where research and building, the fast and the slow meld together. This is always done with a sense of wit and a productive confusion that immerses one in the mystery and humor of the work. Writing about "SNAFUs," the acronym for "Situation Normal All Fucked Up," decorative dilemmas, or an architecture of "surrationalism" comes as easily to Lewis as writing about multivalent performance or mechanical panoramas, where he might delve into the depths of his own work as much as he might explore the work of Luigi Moretti.

In the end, what distinguishes Lewis and LTL from other contemporary practices is their posture toward technology—perhaps even toward speed. The hand is recognizable in their work, but it is not slow. It is extended through drawings into buildings, allowing them to reach numerous scales. Their work is

Clockwise from top left: The ContemporAry Austin - Jones Center exterior (top left) and interior (top right), Austin, TX, USA, 2017 / Claremont University Consortium exterior (middle right) and interior (bottom), Claremont, CA, USA, 2011

Cornell University Upson Hall, Ithaca, NY, USA, 2017

innovative to the extent that it combines the simplicity of material and construction with unique and complex patterns of installation—only afforded through their intense understanding of drawing.

It would be easy to commend a designer whose drawings are seductive. However, the extent to which Lewis and LTL have broken out of the historical trap of the paper-architect is unique. They are a firm that is not only incredibly prolific, but that has also won numerous awards for that work. It is a testament to Lewis's commitment to bringing together an intensity of design research and an intellect to the core of the discipline with a dexterous and uncanny ability see opportunity in every project. It is my pleasure to welcome Paul Lewis.

The ContemporAry Austin - Jones Center, Austin, TX, USA, 2017

LEWIS

AFORMAL ARCHITECTURE

INTRODUCING
JONATHAN SOLOMON

Tonight, we have the unique opportunity to gain insight into Jonathan Solomon's book, *Cities Without Ground* (2012). The notion of a groundless city stems from a strain of architectural fiction and fantasy, owing its discursive roots to *La Città Nuova* (*The New City*, 1914). Drawn at the beginning of the 20th century, it envisioned an incredibly dense, multi-layered city filled with machines and infrastructure. It was Antonio Sant'Elia's visual counterpart to the Futurist Manifesto, which has anchored how architects and urbanists have imagined the city for a

Top and bottom: images from *Cities Without Ground, A Hong Kong Guidebook*, ORO Editions, 2012
Adam Frampton, Jonathon Solomon, and Clara Wong

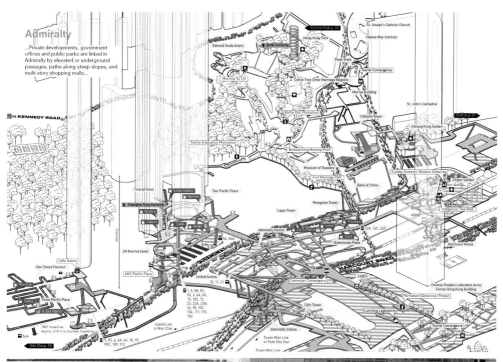

Admiralty

...Private developments, government offices and public parks are linked in Admiralty by elevated or underground passages, paths along steep slopes, and multi-story shopping malls...

hundred years. *La Città Nuova* reflects a deep obsession with speed as well as an obsession with time; where the permanence of architecture dissolves into a chiasma of circulation. In these intense and enthralling drawings, lines of circulation link up every building. There is no datum or street level, merely more layers of circulation along a continuous z-axis of growth; there is no ground. Important to the title of tonight's lecture is this vision conceived by Sant'Elia with an extreme interest in form.

One could argue that in architecture there is a discourse about speed that has evolved over the past hundred years that is "aformal," and perhaps this is at the root of Solomon's lecture this evening. Like apolitical people, aformal architecture may be a way to suggest an increased interest in the speed of exchange and a diminished interest in architecture's representational forms and aesthetics of speed. The temporal and circulatory aspects of architecture and urbanism introduced by *La Città Nuova* continue to capture the imagination of our discourse, speed up architecture, and erode its "groundedness."

One may be inclined to suggest that these types of early modernist speculations shift contemporary intentions away from "Form," with a capital F. Circulatory machinery like escalators and elevators have been tapped by architects for their montage-like programmatic sequences or their capacity to pull pedestrians through the section of a building—turning the cross section into a literal action that displays the thinness and artificiality of ground. In that vein of thinking, the building has "submitted" to circulation. It is no longer clear when you are within circulation or a building, within a building or between buildings, above or below ground. Form is eroded and vaporized.

Only a somewhat curious mind would find fantasy within the mundane and obsessively latch onto the inert characteristics of a city like Hong Kong.

Cities Without Ground, A Hong Kong Guidebook, ORO Editions, 2012
Adam Frampton, Jonathon Solomon, and Clara Wong

By mapping where conditioned environments start and stop in relationship to buildings and their enclosures, and by modeling, drawing, and analyzing the connections and knotted networks of Central and Admiralty, Solomon and his two colleagues, Adam Frampton and Clara Wong, have tapped into the deep roots of urbanity and its emerging 21st-century trends in *Cities Without Ground*.

Solomon's other written works—like his *Pamphlet Architecture* on the Sheridan Expressway and articles with titles such as "Looking for Megastructure: a Partial Archaeology of the Present," "Abhorrent Infrastructure," "Charged Infrastructure," or "Does Your Mall have an Airport," written for *Log* with Max Hirsch—further underpin his fascination with the uncanny and somewhat indeterminable physical and disciplinary boundaries

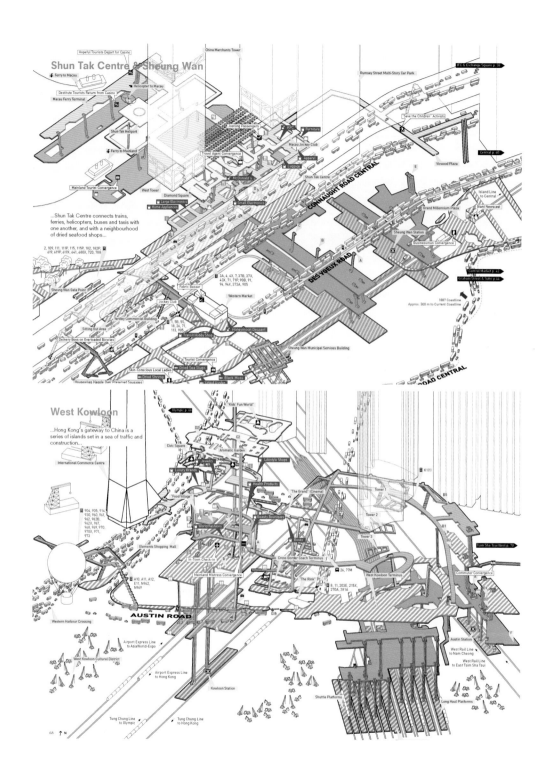

between urban design and architecture; between controlled, conditioned, or formal environments and those that are "aformal," emergent, and not controlled.

This is evident even in some of the small scale built work he has completed as the principal of Solomon Workshop. For example, the folded, red, double-height, opaque storefront and art gallery he completed in Wanchai is carefully calibrated in distinction to its setting—a market street flooded with vendors, people, and tents. Solomon's use of color and texture scale the design to the street and enhance a moody atmosphere of discovery, core to the Hong Kong street market experience; one stumbles into it rather than sees it.

His commitment to collaboration and interdisciplinarity is commendable and is most notable in his editorial works. Among them, *306090*, a journal he started with Emily Abruzzo and Gerald Bodziak, focuses specifically on collaborative and interdisciplinary practices. Where journals often construct their identity as solely theory- or project-based, *306090* reconceives its format, presenting what I regard to be a "book-as-exhibition." Projects are often uniquely developed for each volume. For example, in their issue titled "Making a Case" (2012), 12 international firms designed houses for the publication. The journal not only premiers original work but crosses disciplines—regularly folding fine art into the mix—and bringing together seemingly unrelated or incompatible ideas. Volume 13, "Sustain and Develop" (2010), explores ideas of sustainability in parallel with predominately Chinese trends of development—two ideas that are not necessarily "bedfellows."

Solomon has a willingness to put things together that do not always belong together. This is reflected in his increasingly accomplished role as a curator. "Workshopping; An American Model of Architectural Practice" (2010), the exhibition he co-curated for the Venice Architecture Biennale, brought together successful and accomplished but less discursively important large

Top and bottom: *Cities Without Ground, A Hong Kong Guidebook*, ORO Editions, 2012
Adam Frampton, Jonathon Solomon, and Clara Wong

firms with emerging, discursively important, small, collaborative firms, university labs, and research projects for cities. The basic idea was to generate an implied and literal set of workshops between projects that would otherwise never be in the same room. "Counterpart Cities," which Solomon co-curated with Dorothy Tang for the HKSZ Biennale (2012), put together a combination of consultants, designers, and academics from Hong Kong and Shenzhen to comprise six teams. All original projects conceived by each team, they launched a series of physical obstructions that re-capitulate the flows between the two cities; capturing and slowing down circulation in many cases.

Solomon has been teaching studios and seminars at HKU for the past six years and recently became an associate professor. You will often find his students wandering through Central and Admiralty, captivated by entanglements of architecture and circulation, measuring air temperature or sound. Solomon is astute in observing his surroundings, which extends beyond his ability to find unique collaborations and into his interpretations of his physical surroundings; finding the "misfits" and things that do not neatly fit into our discursive histories the most interesting. His obsession with circulation reflects an interest in odd scales of architecture and its potential aformal qualities. This is somewhat uncomfortable territory in the discipline. Simply suggesting that architecture can be "aformal" calls into question the role of design, form, and ultimately speed. In Solomon's case, it also seems to move between disciplines, between the city and architecture, between public and private space.

Uncomfortable things are often the most learned and Solomon's work promises to crack open fertile ground for architecture, not only in the context of Hong Kong but in the broader framework of cities and their intrinsic environments.

It is my pleasure to welcome Jonathan Solomon.

Cities Without Ground, A Hong Kong Guidebook, ORO Editions, 2012
Adam Frampton, Jonathon Solomon, and Clara Wong

44

THE SUBJECT OF MEGALOPOLIS

INTRODUCING
ALBERT POPE

There are few people in architecture who can boast about their book selling out, let alone whose work is sought out for over 15 years by a steady stream of academics and leaders in the field. While he would never admit it, with his book *Ladders* (1996) Albert Pope has done just this.

Pope is an "architect's architect." For those of us who have struggled with urbanism—in particular, the blight of American urbanism—this book and his voice stand apart. On_Speed, the theme of this lecture series, sets up several possible turns and oppositions within our discourse. One of

Albert Pope, *Ladders*, 1996

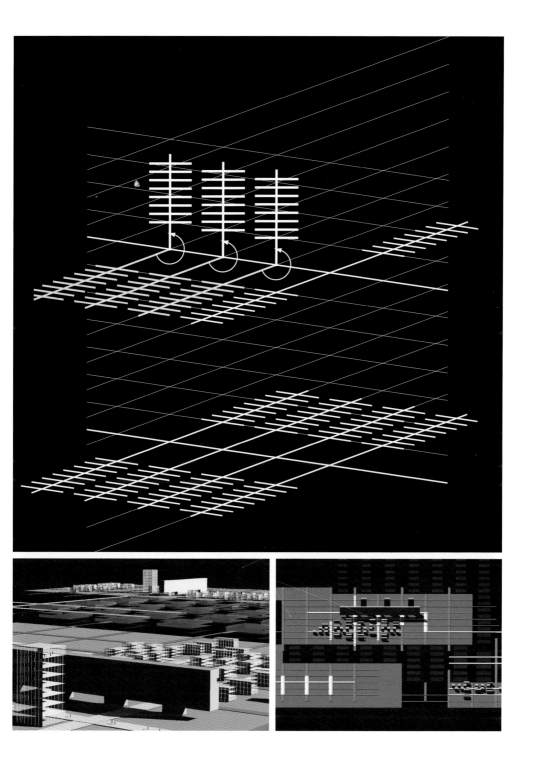

them is the death of form. In other words, speed can kill form. Recurrent in the discourse is the notion that as urban networks, freeways, Internet cables, material, information, and pedestrian flows become smoother and faster, these networks will overtake and eradicate form. The suggestion speculates that we will have informal (or possibly aformal, as discussed in previous lectures) cities, emergent from the bottom up, and all we have to do as architects is tap into that aformality.

On one level, speed can deeply threaten architecture, a practice which by its nature must argue for "Form" with a capital F. Terms like "sprawl" are borne out of this disciplinary anxiety. Speed characterizes the formless urban diaspora that results from a primacy of circulation. Freeways and lines of continuity slice through an otherwise "proper" urban form, leaving massive gaps. Sprawl is a term used by those against it. This phrasing keeps the formal definition of sprawl ambiguous, inducing a propensity in the discipline to nostalgically argue for the legibility of earlier (typically European) form in cities. On another level, perhaps one should be cautious about those architects who suggest they are able to design the formless; those who suggest they can embrace sprawl. There is a certain psychosis in suggesting that one can make form out of that which it is not, and typically these projects result in more form or picturesque analogues of the formless.

Pope's work takes the issue of form in the city on directly; not by suggesting that form goes away or nostalgically arguing for some lost type of urban form, but by simply suggesting that form is no longer the primary agent of urban

Pope's work takes the issue of form in the city on directly; not by suggesting that form goes away or nostalgically arguing for some lost type of urban form, but by simply suggesting that form is no longer the primary agent of urban growth.

48

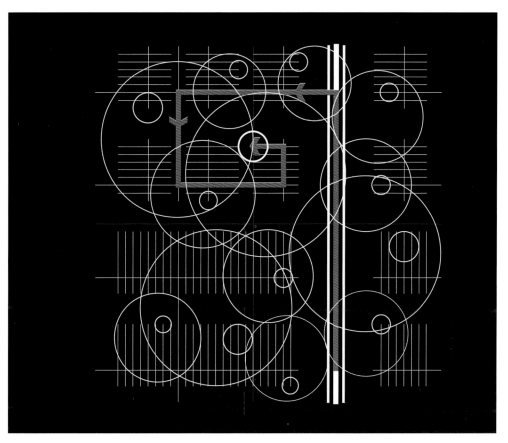

Albert Pope, *Ladders*, 1996

growth. To this extent, Pope's work is quite innovative; the form he speaks of is both novel and an intrinsic part of the city. His writings are a direct affront to the very difficult balance between speed, time, space, and form.

He has brilliantly discussed how modern urbanism—contrary to common assumption—is involved in the production of closed systems; where they are historically presumed to be "free" and open in plan. Pope's book *Ladders* transforms the incredibly familiar grid into something you have never seen before. It has centripetal and centrifugal characteristics. There are spirals, ellipsis, archipelagos, and, as the title suggests, ladders; a fragment of grid-

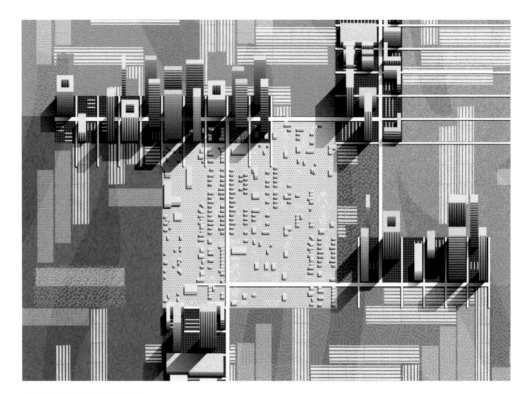

Albert Pope, *Ladders*, 1996

form within what he calls a "City of Space." The ladder becomes a tool that gives us eyes on the "sub-urban," agglomerations that are subordinate to the mainstream of our discourse.

Posing as simple, didactic, black and white diagrams sprinkled throughout the book, each of Pope's drawings has an air of visual illusionism. He performs exercises on the grid before our eyes, turning a plane of continuity and openness—subtly nipped and tucked—into a closed discontinuous system. It makes you rub your eyes, thinking someone is playing a trick on you. The project is crucial to anyone living in a dense city or studying urbanism. As Pope suggests, "if the city cannot be thought, it ceases to be an object of collective or individual concern."

This is a particularly unique point of view because, for Pope, thinking is designing. They are not separate acts. And, if you ever get your hands on a copy of *Ladders*, the humble, diagrammatic insertions buried within the book are an arsenal of unassuming secret weapons that one by one crack away at our very presumptions about urbanity. Pope seems less interested in the traditions of urbanism and more in what draws us into the city, the fragmentary sloppiness of density and urbanity.

His roles as both an academic and writer reflect the profound thoughtfulness and individuality of his work. Articles with titles such as "Divided Megalopolis," "The Invention of Space," "The Space of Invention," "Block of Space," and "Ex Nihilo Urbanism" showcase Pope's ability to upend our assumptions about the things that are seemingly familiar. He redefines space or the megalopolis, making him both provocateur and designer, instigator and possible savior.

51

The holes and gaps between traditional forms are key to his understanding of urbanism and its opportunities for architects. This is not only apparent in his writings but also in his architectural work, where the void becomes an instrument of design. His Wroxton Road Townhouses pose as a somewhat familiar row of brick houses in a Houston neighborhood. However, they are not only the densest architecture on their block, they simultaneously intervene at the block's scale. The simple, rectilinear, flat-roofed form is subdivided and undone. It is a "group-form," intricately laced with voids in all axis. As one moves up and down the stairs of the units, the gaps within, between, through, and across programs become your primary experience. North American architects often recognize that you eat in your bedroom and work in your kitchen; and therein lies the problem with didactically programming a house. In Wroxton, assemblies of voids emerging out of the stairs produce virtual torques and ellipses, flowing within and between units. The voids not only make those types of programmatic inversions vital but also give each unit a palpable relationship to the block in which it sits.

Through his engagement of the void as urban form via the different modalities of his practice and scales of his projects, Pope opens our eyes to the Megalopolis and invents new subjects within it; coursing through it and expanding our understanding of its speeds and forms.

It is my pleasure to welcome Albert Pope.

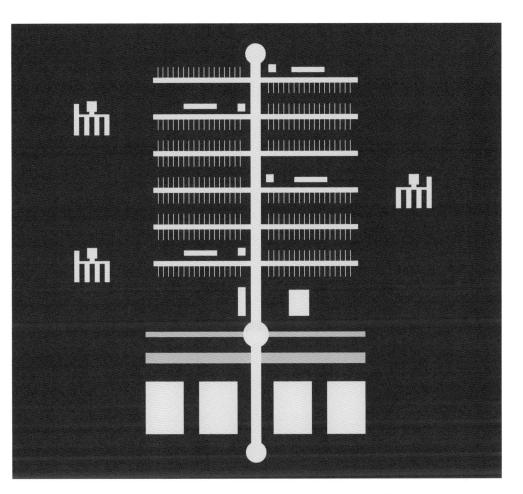

Albert Pope, *Ladders*, 1996

INTRODUCING
MICHAEL YOUNG

Scale is the primary difference between product design and architecture. As much as architects attempt to speed up their buildings with software and throw a lot of prototyping equipment at them, the scale of architecture and its requisite economies make clear that buildings cannot be fully prototyped or constructed in the same way a piece of furniture, glassware, appliance, bike, or car is made. We may not be able to go that fast! By implication, architecture must deal with mixtures of processes and materials-assemblies that combine high tech and low tech, modeling and

Corian Design Studio, Shanghai, China, 2010

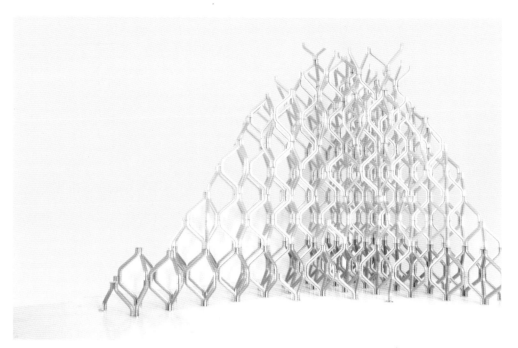

Zipte Link, 2009

prototyping, standard construction with digitally fabricated construction. The dream of mass-producing architecture, while perhaps more technologically tenable today than it was 50 years ago, is still encumbered by its cultural, economic, political, and social parameters. Too often it is presumed that because we use the same types of software and equipment to model, test, and prototype there are a lot of overlaps between industrial design and architecture. However, this overlooks the issue of scale and does not recognize the autonomy of each discipline.

This presumption perpetuates the (somewhat antiquated) Renaissance idea that architects can wear multiple hats and be industrial designers; as much as industrial designers might think they can easily become architects—either of which may lead to a questionable erosion of expertise. In addition, they neglect to recognize the necessary and productive difference of disciplines and professions.

The frame is no longer a single line but a multivalent geometry. It is no longer continuous and sealed, but like a window aperture, it opens to receive other components.

It is clear, however, that we share similar problems and that those can open doors between the disciplines. Among these opportunities is the issue of multiplicity. Even though we may be working at different scales we share the problem of having to incorporate other, standardized elements into our design. Instead of elements like windows and doors into buildings, industrial designers must negotiate how to incorporate legs and handles into products. How elements are combined and integrated within a design is what often distinguishes one designer from another, and what makes a design more or less innovative; be it architectural design or industrial design.

Today, one might suggest that there is a propensity in both industrial design and architectural design to smooth out all of these elemental differences. However, for Michael Young there is a clear intention to absorb ulterior elements, giving his work a vitality and sensibility that distinguishes it from others. In each of the two bicycles he has designed for Giant, there is very little exposed hardware—common in much of Young's work. The frames are designed to smoothly transition between truss, stem, and fork. These moves may seemingly contradict my prior statement and lead one to believe that singularity, smoothness, and full integration are the goals of his design.

However, upon closer inspection, the bike frame works more three-dimensionally than most to integrate an intense amount of peripheral, standardized hardware, ranging from headlights and taillights to bike locks. The frame is no longer a single line but a multivalent geometry. It is no longer continuous and sealed, but like a window aperture, it opens to receive other components. The design allows for other elements to be inserted within it and at the same time recapitulates them in new ways. As Young puts it, he wanted

57

to design a bike that, "did not look like some designer's fantasy, but must hold its own at a bike show."

To accomplish this degree of innovation, one must be deeply involved in the production process, work directly with the manufacturers to develop custom "tools," and go through an immense number of prototypes and iterations. Young's move from England to Taiwan and then to Hong Kong reflects his commitment and desire to get his hands dirty on the factory floor and to develop strong collaborations with engineers and fabricators.

Performance is a key ingredient in Young's work and not only in its functional dimension. His designs exhibit another aspect of performance, where their ability to resituate familiar elements in unfamiliar ways makes his designs productively intriguing, mysterious, and interactive. As he puts it, there is a "constant questioning of typologies and habits" that drives his work.

This is most notable in the projects Young has done with Tittot, DuPont, and EOQ. These projects showcase Young's truly unique capabilities to experiment and develop design research; in some cases, without an end-product in mind. These three projects not only harness the resources of manufacturing in the Pearl River Delta and China but also showcase Young's ability to develop work that draws upon the history of Chinese ornament and texture; using their conceptual underpinnings to develop contemporary ideas about design. His book *Works in China* (2011) reflect the fact he is not only committed to working in China, but also committed to ensuring his designs "work" in China—to give them cultural value.

The numerous prototypes and material tests that lie behind the final products show a deep understanding of design and reflect a belief that one learns the most from the objects one makes.

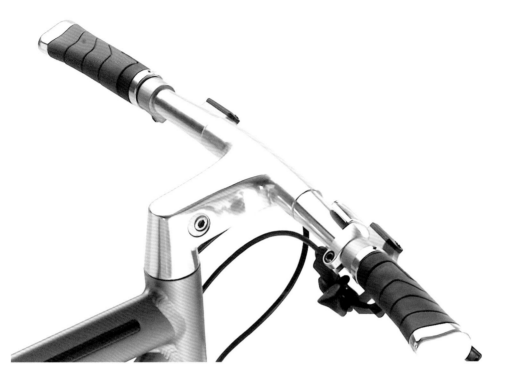

City Speed, Giant, 2009

The delirious, algorithmically sequenced textures he has been experimenting with (found in both the Tittot glassware and the DuPont showroom projects) feature how traditional Chinese appliqué becomes three-dimensional. Two-dimensional patterns become three-dimensional textures, integrating stands and handles.

Young's ability to take normative material processes to new levels is further reflected in his Zipte Link project for EOQ where he rethinks the tubular aluminum extrusion. "Fluting" the stem and bending it into subtle S-shaped elements, the extrusion becomes a structural lattice, adapting to multiple scales that congeal to become a wall-screen or a table; an interesting balance between a standardized, "kit-of-parts," domestic infrastructure, and the personalization of a dwelling via furniture.

Young has a ferocious appetite for experimentation and is also involved directly in the production of his work; he is "on the floor," so-to-speak. The numerous prototypes and material tests that lie behind the final products show a deep understanding of design and reflect a belief that one learns the most from the objects one makes. While his rate of production has a speed-like acumen architects might envy or associate with industrial design, his thoroughness and hands-on approach couples that output with a depth of focus and deceleration akin to architecture and its lengthy design to production timelines.

A natural outcome of this approach is the design of architecturally laden environments. Young has recently started designing interiors, including the Chivas Regal Bar for the HK Art Fair and Pissarro Dining in Central; and forayed into architecture, designing a fictitious tower, both extending his research into different scales and poking fun at the promotional promiscuity of architects.

Each of his projects takes something very simple and develops, re-works, and refines it. He seems to be less interested in re-inventing the entire system than in understanding it, tweaking it, and transforming it. Young's ability to combine both the familiar and the unfamiliar, to combine rapid production with intense focus is truly unique. The result is formal, materially adept, and, perhaps most of all, situational. The work interacts with the body or our perceived protocols of use to resituate our habits. While there are different scales of operation and expertise between architecture and industrial design, Young's work also showcases several critical shared interests; multiplicity and performance among them. He has a gentle way of prying open opportunities for design within a culture which may otherwise not recognize its value: China. He works at two speeds, at once using the best of China today and projecting it forward into new modalities of thinking and production. In a sense, he works both in China and on China—something valuable for all of us to hear more about. It is my pleasure to welcome Michael Young.

Michael Young for Tittot, 2010

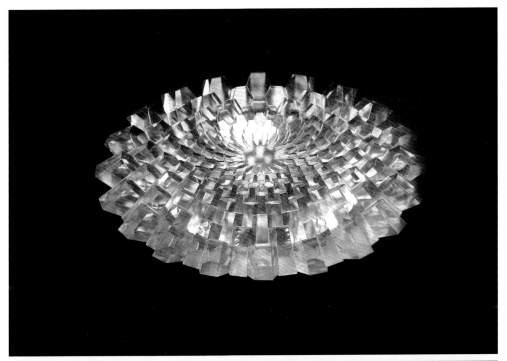

POWER OF PLACE

INTRODUCING
KENGO KUMA

Within the context of this lecture series, On_Speed, some may be wondering how a lecture with a title like "Power of Place" fits in. The notion of "place" is innately against the international; it is about locality and one can presume slowness. Speed, however, has as much to do with acceleration as deceleration. In the work of Kengo Kuma and Associates one sees both happening simultaneously. The materiality of the work has a sensibility that is pertinent to architecture discourse. There are unique combinations of both virtual and real materials, local and non-

Clockwise from top left: Teahouse, Beijing, China, 2014 / Lotus House, East Japan, 2005 / Opposite House, Beijing, China, 2008 / Krug x Kuma, Tokyo, Japan, 2005 / Sanlitun Soho, Beijing, China, 2010

The work induces an ambiguous state
of materiality similar to fog, a state
between a liquid and a gas.

local materials, and assemblies that subtly pixelate between opacity and transparency. I would suggest that the work operates at "variable speeds of materiality."

Materiality is a confusing word in architectural discourse. Some people may associate architects who speak of materiality as those who align themselves with modernist moral imperatives that enunciate the "truth and honesty" of materials. Others may believe that materiality is about "essence" and a return to "the natural." However, architecture is often about the combination of materials and the qualities those assemblies produce. Architectural materiality (with an emphasis on the "-ity") is an effect produced by the designer. The materiality of a piece of architecture may result in different appearances, ranging from monolithic permanence to ephemeral transparency. In either case, any architect who tinkers with materiality must be deeply devoted to understanding the behaviors of materials, the tolerances of their construction, and foresee how those materials affect space.

Few architects in the history of the discipline have devoted their careers to this endeavor more ferociously than Kengo Kuma. Coining the term "material structures," requiring the discipline at large to no longer separate structure and material, and often referring to his buildings as "filters" or "arrays of particles," Kuma's work stands out because of its unique stance within the discourse on materiality. Although his book *Anti-Object* (2013) supports early career polemical claims he made about his desire to erase buildings, as the work has matured it suggests something even more provocative; a building's unstable perception between appearing and disappearing. The work induces an ambiguous state of materiality similar to fog, a state between a liquid and a gas.

64

Chokkura Plaza and Shelter. Tochigi, Japan, 2006

While Kuma works with many natural materials, such as wood and stone, he often works with them in "unnatural" ways. Slicing prefabricated concrete hollow core slabs to expose their porosity, slicing stone so thin that you can almost see through it, or using local stone that is nearly falling apart and not meant for building construction, combining it with steel as a structural element, Kuma seems to enjoy ways in which his buildings may subtly jar typical associations. Heavy stone becomes light and airy; steel becomes "foamy." His intimacy with materials results less in a moral imperative and more in creative sprints that allow him to work with material in composite and synthetic ways.

This facility with materials pushes Kuma's work away from the natural and into the preternatural. Architectural ideas like "blurring" or "dissolving" are unique in Kuma's work where they perfectly encapsulate that state between

Xinjin Zhi Museum, Chengdu, China, 2011

the object and the non-object. Many of his projects use intensely layered structural/cladding systems that make it nearly impossible to tell where the enclosure lies. You see a great breadth of ways in which he experiments with textures, layers, and screens; through several projects and at different scales. He couples these test cases with a multitude of techniques, ranging from gradients to pixelation, making the work difficult to categorize. It is precisely this dexterity, breadth of material research, and experimentation that makes Kuma one of the most distinguished architects right now. Projects like the Chokkura Plaza and Shelter (2006), which uses a stone and steel structure to turn the building into a porous gradient, showcase how unique Kuma's multivalent approach is.

Acclaimed both inside Japan and around the world, Kengo Kuma and Associates has received numerous international awards where each project

Xinjin Zhi Museum, Chengdu, China, 2011

often uses new materials to explore traditional cultural environments and rituals. Among them are inflatable teahouses, a teahouse made of post office boxes, or pavilions comprised of new composites like shape memory alloys; juxtaposing new and old, craft and machine.

Kengo Kuma and Associates has placed first in numerous competitions ranging from museums to master plans in Japan, China, Taiwan, the Middle East, and Europe. The Xinjin Zhi Museum (2011) in Chengdu extrapolates on some of their previous work with stone, magnifying the material to new levels of lightness. Among other built master plans and developments, Sanlitun Soho (2010) in Beijing is a residential and office complex that builds upon ideas of color saturation and layering that were earlier developed in their acclaimed Opposite House Hotel (2008), which is part of the same district.

His intimacy with materials results less in a moral imperative and more in creative sprints that allow him to work with material in composite and synthetic ways.

Educated in both the United States and Japan, Kuma has a unique perspective on architecture and is a prolific writer and critic. As a post graduate student, he and a group of colleagues, known as Gruppo Specio, were writing regular articles for the magazine *Space Design* that were among the first to track and critique the complex and combined influences of the contemporary Japanese architecture scene. He has since written numerous books. Among them is *Anti-Object*, which was originally published in Japan, then re-published eight years later by the Architectural Association in London. Ten monographs have followed his work since 1997, edited by colleagues from both Japan and Europe. Even in his writings, project descriptions, and in published drawings you are aware of an obsession with the thickness of the material—down to the millimeter—and a precision about how those materials are deployed.

Kuma can work with history and tradition in contemporary ways. This is a very tricky line few can pull off, I suspect even more tricky in Japan than in Hong Kong or North America. His work as an educator reflects his commitment to being able to walk that tight rope, to find an ease within various cultural contradictions, and develop work out of them. The Water / Glass House (1995) is one clear example of this, where Kuma builds upon the complex layers of Japanese architectural history by finding contemporary ideas in Bruno Taut's Hyuga Villa (1936), which Taut based on Katsura Imperial Villa (17th century) in Kyoto; insinuating an endless and potent circle of discourse, history, and contemporaneity.

Top: Xinjin Zhi Museum, Chengdu, China, 2011
Bottom: Hoshinosato Annex, Yamaguchi, Japan, 2005

68

Kuma has the unique ability to develop a distinct materiality, and has a willingness to work with new and old materials, literal and virtual. His invention of terms like "digital gardening" or "material structures" all reflect a critical, curious, and deeply committed aptitude to explore one's work. Over his distinguished career, he has shown that he is not easily swayed by popular trends, while at the same time he has been open to evolving his work to address contemporary issues. The coarse mixture of traditional materials and their synthetic counterpart, between history and contemporaneity, and between acceleration and deceleration allow Kuma to rethink terms like "place" with a freshness and criticality that opens up their future potentials rather than abiding by their historical underpinnings. I look forward to seeing how these themes relate to the "Power of Place."

Please join me in welcoming Kengo Kuma.

Water / Glass, Shizuoka, Japan / 1995

SOCIAL ENRICHMENT

INTRODUCING
ANDREW BROMBERG

Nestled within Aedas, Andrew Bromberg has been churning out innovative work that challenges our assumptions about practice, the autonomy of architecture, and what the term "convention" means within the discipline. Designing an impressive quiver of projects that range in scale and location, his work stands out as among the first to be both borne out of and designed to encapsulate the speed of production and building in Asia today.

Clockwise from top: The Star, exterior and interior, Singapore, 2012 / Hong Kong West Kowloon Station, Hong Kong, 2018 / Langham Place, Guangzhou, China, 2013

The Star, Singapore, 2012

Architecture of speed is not typically something one might affiliate with "Social Enrichment," the title of Bromberg's lecture. Where speed tends to gloss over and smooth out with the goal of profit as its end, social enrichment is about nurturing, taking notice, and being attentive to one's surroundings for the sake of social well-being; it is slow. As a broader project, Bromberg's work seems to miraculously contain both aspects, understanding each respective speed (fast and slow) as equally valuable, directly fabricating both into the form, details, and materials of his designs.

Contemporary architecture discourse and practice still suffers from certain strains of what one might call a "modernist hangover." None is perhaps more elusive than the desire to unify all parts within the whole of a design. From the detail to the mass, there is an overt bias in the discipline toward wholism. This bias has produced a schism in the discipline and within the profession. There are architects who discuss and legitimize their buildings from the social

Each project vibrates between being a dispersal of individual masses and simultaneously amasses into one collective architecture.

forces that make up its "site" and "program," as if the design was inevitable; "it is this way because of these forces." And there are architects who use disciplinary autonomy and novelty to add critical value to (and to legitimize) their moves; making their designs one of a kind. Star architects, commercial and corporate architects alike commonly fall prey to either one of these approaches and tend to assign moral value within one or the other; within monumentalist "object"-making or social "field"-making. One is abstract and disengaged, the other is real and engaged. One is modular and generic, the other is specific and about the place. One is profitable, the other is not, and so on.

For an architect like Bromberg one can see a frustration with, or at least the recognition of, the inadequacies of either approach. This could be in part because he has invented a new type of practice. Instead of being the traditional design figurehead of a corporate firm who establishes its overall brand identity and gives it coherence, Bromberg's role is more tactical. His studio exists within Aedas, one of the largest firms in the world); similar to the way Skunk Works is an R+D arm of the U.S. military or Miramax films was the independent film house for Disney. Bromberg uses the technological prowess, power, and structure of Aedas to leverage trust and encourage clients to take risks on new ideas.

Bromberg has a sensibility that allows his architecture to absorb market forces, developer-based criteria, and commercialism as much as he allows his designs to absorb forms of avant-gardism, extreme form, and explore the social welfare of place-making. There is a huge range of experimentation within the work, which one must admire simply in sheer volume and quantity. What is even more unique is the type of rigor that seems to organize

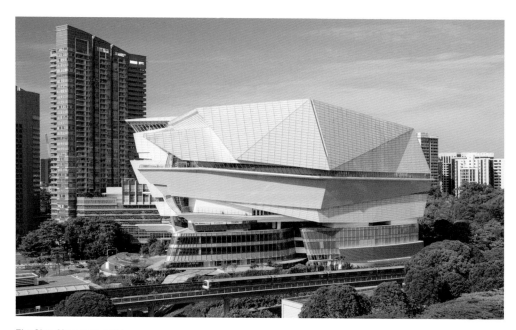

The Star, Singapore, 2012

Bromberg's work. The projects are "loose;" they have a compelling playfulness which gives them an ad hoc character. They seem to advocate less for visual or aesthetic rigor (common in a world of speed, where there is a necessity for efficiency and repetition) and are more invested in new forms of architectural "coherence." Each project vibrates between being a dispersal of individual masses and simultaneously amasses into one collective architecture.

Using meticulously crafted modeling algorithms, the projects activate the space around and between elements. They form an urban and architectural coherence that is otherwise a chiasma of circulatory, programmatic, and developer-driven trajectories operating with autonomous and opposing agendas. In many ways, Bromberg's projects both register the speeds of those forces and subvert them; slow them down and disperse them.

Langham Place, Guangzhou, China, 2013

The Star (2012) in Singapore brings together precisely these kinds of oppositional forces. It is at once a mall and a major civic icon. The architectural experience ranges from a Piranesi-like civic plaza with a forest of columns permeating the contours of retail circulation to an exfoliating bowl-theater with seats swirled around a stage. All the environmental, commercial and structural constraints are computationally indexed in architectural elements; separated, exposed and put on display. This bundle of elements penetrates through the interior as much as it hemorrhages outward. The complex fluctuates between readings. It is at once two or more buildings and one building; at once an outdoor plaza and an enclosed civic box. The partially open-air sectional space between the car park and the theater holds the project together. As Bromberg puts it, you can "crawl under, move through, traverse around, or climb onto" the complex. It is coming apart at the seams as much as it is being held together.

Acclaimed projects like the Hong Kong West Kowloon Station (2018) or the Nanfung Commercial Hospitality and Exhibition Complex (2013) take architectural cohesion to a higher level. Each pushes elements further apart—across city blocks—and plays with an even more diverse set of typologies between podium and tower. Bromberg has designed over 60 projects with his 11-year-old studio at Aedas. The projects are an index of the global hot spots of architecture, including Hong Kong, China, Southeast Asia, Taiwan, the Middle East, India, and Russia. They range in scale, size, and use, spanning the gamut from mixed use, commercial, residential, hotel and resort, civic, and cultural programs; not to mention the spectrum of typologies of work ranging from master planning to infrastructure and airport projects.

Bromberg has a humble personality that is reflective of Southeast Asian (and particularly Cantonese) culture. His persona augments his ability to find architectural opportunities within local, regional, and international opportunities across an array of complexities one might encounter in the contemporary commercial and speed-driven culture of practice. Like that culture, there is a vested interest in getting the buildings to "work," giving them an agency and using a dense amount of technology to explore this effect

The Star, Singapore, 2012

and its social impacts. A testament to this is that the projects are often at once commercially, socially, and critically successful.

Contouring, curving, or swirling (among numerous inventions one might find in a Bromberg Aedas project) are neither gratuitous nor are they entirely subservient to convention. Bromberg and his team subtly tweak pro-formas and the rules of the design to a point where the design is nearly at odds with itself. His talent lies in his ability to reel out these differences just far enough to pull them back in; to design spaces that may not be coherent as much as they imbue a sense of architectural cohesion. This approach to design reflects a willingness to take risks and a thoughtfulness that seems to place value on urbanity—on the mood and the soul of the city, on the state between order and disorder, between object and field. Perhaps this is Bromberg's concoction for "Social Enrichment."

Please join me in welcoming Andrew Bromberg.

MATERIALISM

INTRODUCING
YUNG HO CHANG

"Materialism," the topic of this evening's lecture, is a precarious topic in architectural discourse and at large. It can reflect both a cultural narcissism—the materialism of consuming goods—as much as it can elicit metaphysical ways of understanding our natural surroundings as nothing but matter and energy. Yung Ho Chang's work seems to involve both forms of materialism, dealing with ideas of cultural value bound to materials as much as the work exhibits a physical understanding of its

Clockwise from top left: Vertical Glass House, Shanghai, China, 2013 / Jishou University Research and Education Building, Jishou China, 2006 / Gwangju Biennale Bamboo Lantern, 2008 / The Bay, Qingpu District, Shanghai, China, 2010

The Bay, Qingpu District, Shanghai, China, 2010

surroundings. The thick, diffused spatial textures of Chang's work can be seen as a radical rethinking of architectural space. The projects often shift conventional solid and void relationships into a blurry state. In many cases, the interaction between matter and energy, mass and space are pushed to extremes. There is simultaneously an embedded awareness about specific materials and techniques, and there is an attentiveness to their meaning and cultural value. Weaving is used in several projects; however not as an idea limited to its conventional material scale and within the micro articulation of surfaces. It also appears at a much larger scale where it is used as a device to explore weaving between masses. Traditional materials may be used but their articulation is anything but typical. They are often artificially transformed, for example, from that which is heavy to unnatural states of lightness. These counterintuitive, composited, and overlapping interests informing the work produce a truly "unusual architecture," as his studio's namesake, Feichang

There is simultaneously an embedded
awareness about specific materials and
techniques, and there is an attentiveness
to their meaning and cultural value.

Jianzhu or FCJZ, insinuates. His work is at once located and local, and
dislocated and global.

Often in contemporary architecture discourse (and certainly within the
regional and global political realm) the rural is pitted against the urban as
much as vernacular against modern and slow against fast. This innuendo and
these themes actively underpin Chang's work. However, the divide between
urban and rural, local and international, fast and slow may not be so clear.
One could argue that this presumed and somewhat artificial separation noted
in western architectural histories (and its political corollaries) is the most
ambiguous in China. Artifacts like the Tilling and Weaving illustrations and
poems of the Qing Dynasty and Kangxi Emperor make clear that agriculture
was seen as an "instrument" of the state, laden with overtones of pre-
modernity and industrialization. More to the point, this "guide" for rural life
does not parse the machine and the landscape, work and recreation, or even
necessarily the urban and rural. The collection of poems and illustrations
points to a vitality of modalities that co-exist as domestic, professional, and
ecological practices that are at once synthetic and natural, rural as much as
they are urban, civic as much as they are domestic. The ambiguity about what
is and was urban, and what is and was rural is a thread that might be traced
through Chang's architectural work, his personal history, and his broader
career.

Texture and scale are undercurrents in Chang's work that not only reinforce
the great diversity of projects he has completed but also which make his
work innovative and important within the context of this discussion on speed.
Many of his projects showcase a breaking down of scale that allows both "the
monumental" and "the intricate" to coexist. Under one large roof, a residence

83

is broken into an arrangement of three smaller, somewhat autonomous residences: Is it one building or four? Repeatedly, this contrast of scale shows up in his designs, whether it is a small or large project, interior, ground up, or a renovation. This technique of placing buildings within buildings produces odd inversions of typology and scale: rooms within cities, cities within landscapes, landscapes within buildings. Splitting, perforating, weaving, and nesting texture is something found not only in Chang's split concrete faces or innovative wall-screens, limiting it to literal materialities. It is equally evident that one can understand texture as an architectural effect that results from the displacement of scales, and simultaneous diffusion and contrast of interior and exterior spaces, opening up new possibilities for understanding the term "materiality."

As the work with his studio has evolved, one sees evidence of this technique being pushed to even greater extremes of experimentation. Projects like the Corporate Headquarters for the software company Ufida and the Jishou University Complex, both completed in 2006, show how this combination of ideas becomes a model for planning at a larger scale. Ufida is a relatively simple square mass "drenched" with perforations at multiple scales. The taut enclosure, mixed with punched-hole openings, cantilevered masses, and courtyards, shifts from smooth to coarse as one moves around the project and deeper into its interior. The Jishou University Complex reworks a podium and tower typology. Using a course texture of wooden "barnacles" that protrude from roofs and dangle from the face of the tower, the project erodes distinctions between horizontal and vertical. Both projects are at once large and delicate, both reflect and diffuse into their surroundings as much as they develop new interiors displaced within an existing landscape.

Many of his projects showcase a breaking down of scale that allows both "the monumental" and "the intricate" to coexist.

Tang Palace Restaurant, Hangzhou, China, 2010

Like a good actor, Yung Ho Chang has avoided the trappings of being typecast and has used the diversity of his work to his advantage. It is astounding to see the volume of work FCJZ has completed. Even more impressive is the range, spanning from residential, commercial, retail, university, arts institutions, corporate headquarters, and housing to table wear, furniture, exhibition, and pavilion design. Unique among his colleagues around the world, his design research is fantastically circular. Ideas prototyped and tested for something as small as his studio's bathroom become a landscape installation, then might evolve into interior designs or building designs or back into product designs.

In some of his more recent works, like the Shanghai Corporate Pavilion for World Expo 2010, the Tang Place restaurant in Hangzhou, and his Bamboo Lantern for the Gwangju Biennale, texture and the interplay of scales releases innovative ideas about figuration, perception, and synthetic and natural

Ufida, Beijing, China, 2006

materials. Each project amplifies the idea of a building within a building. Figures are contradictory: curvilinear inside of rectilinear, spheres inside of cubes, a collection of containers within a larger container. This "figural offset" places pressure on the interstitial spaces, which in each case are the most lush, savory, and surprising parts of the projects. For example, in Tang Place dropped ceilings are transformed into an enchanting, forest-like collection of VIP pods.

In each of these three projects there is an uncanny veiling effect where mass appears and disappears. Local materials, like bamboo, are mixed and laminated with more synthetic materials. Other media like lighting, video, or water are embedded within components, walls, or ceilings, augmenting the dynamic and fluctuating perceptions of the projects. It is abundantly clear that the work's physical characteristics and cultural values resist clear, stable readings.

CHANG

Ufida, Beijing, China, 2006

This rigor of design research, breadth, and diversity of scales could only be the artifact of a curious intellect. Chang's career reflects his work. It is as much about location as dislocation. He positioned himself early on as someone working out of the local context of Beijing, while being simultaneously engaged in global discourse networks. Not only was FCJZ the first private architecture office in Beijing, but Chang was also one of the first major exports of Chinese architecture to the United States. Chang is a rare species where he not only studied in both China and the U.S., receiving his Masters from Berkeley, but continued to go back and forth and thrive in both contexts. He is the former head of the architecture department at MIT and simultaneously the founding head of the Graduate Center for Architecture at Peking University.

It is easy to admire and be impressed by Chang's architectural and academic achievements, his ability to work in multiple contexts, as well as it is to appreciate his humble demeanor and his unforgettable smile. However, it is the "unusual" aspect of his work that I find the most compelling. I believe the work is truly unusual because things like texture evolve into a broader idea about context and scale. Perhaps most profound is the fact that Chang's work suggests that the void is in fact matter; it is articulated and enmeshed into the massing of each project to create deliriously rich spaces that no longer distinguish between solid and void, small and large, rural or urban. To his credit, these differences are not architecturally smoothed out, but inlaid; they have an oscillating rhythm and texture. Within the context of this lecture series I would posit that what is important about Chang's work is that it has an "oscillating speed." His projects breed contrasts where scales, textures, and materials play off one another, allowing for new forms of perception and experience to emerge. Perhaps this is one way of understanding his "materialism?" I look forward to finding out.

Please join me in welcoming Yung Ho Chang.

Top: The Shanghai Corporate Pavilion, Shanghai, China, 2010
Bottom: The Bay, Qingpu District, Shanghai, China, 2010

THE POSSIBLE
IMPOSSIBILITY

INTRODUCING
WOLF D. PRIX

On_Speed, the title of this series when it was launched in Spring of 2012, saw many instantiations of what architectural speed might involve. Wolf Prix and his practice Coop Himmelb(l)au expand that idea further and in some cases quite literally. Given the repute of the firm, which is known for favoring random accidents of design that occur during stages of drug-induced charrettes, one might conclude that Prix's inclusion in this series was to advocate for the "recreational" or "experimental" side of speed; a trajectory best left to the minds of the audience or readers to speculate

Clockwise from top left: Musée des Confluences, Lyon, France, 2014 / UFA Cinema Center, Dresden, Germany, 1998 / Busan Cinema Center, Busan, South Korea, 2012 / BMW Welt, Munich, Germany, 2007

Dalian International Conference Center, Dalian, China, 2012

upon. Certainly, we cannot deny the "bad boy," Jimmy Hendrix infatuated patina that Prix and Himmelb(l)au propagate as an ethos, method, and means to architectural design.

However, I would like to offer a more sober and disciplinary angle on the work, which makes it relevant to the academy, to our contemporary condition as a profession, and to a series with this title. The optics of speed are blurry. Unlike velocity, which solely accounts for the rate of motion but could go nowhere, speed has to account for the distance traveled. Prix's work is not kinematic, has no "giant robots" installed in it, and does not actually move. While often saturated with graphics and media that animate and provoke alternative perceptions of the buildings, the projects are not necessarily in motion. These mediums augment the architecture brilliantly, but these attributes lean more toward velocity and are not the most pertinent to Himmelb(l)au's work, when exploring its contributions to a discourse on speed.

Delicately balanced to the point of falling or breaking, and flooded with line work, Prix's projects often have the sense they are about to move. It is not a polite implication, but one that is on the verge of threatening, as if it might fall on top of you or engulf you. While one could understand this affect as alienating, there is something mysteriously inviting about how these masses of structure—often rendered as heavy, thick, and torqued—buoyantly fly over you. Like a surfer going into the tube of a wave or a skier dropping into a steep mountain chute, the buildings entrance and lull you in as much as they go against the grain of your culturally inscribed understanding of "entry," or perhaps your inscribed notion of safety. Because of their implied motion, the projects often heighten your attentiveness to their surroundings, augment adrenaline levels and result in a set of neuromodulated affects in their subjects; the effects of the brain when stimulated by endorphins.

To induce an experience of speed in this manner one has to have an acute understanding of the center of gravity of the things they design and how to tinker with them such that those centers implicitly collapse on the inhabitant, agitating their haptic and sensorial experience. Prix's work demonstrates this in an astonishingly artful manner. The mash up of separate masses— orthogonal and curvilinear often nearly touching or interpenetrated— heightens the texture and density the experience, making it seem like you have traveled a greater distance than you actually have.

The circulation is often on display (showing the speeds of Prix's buildings) as much as it ingrains the visitor in the spectacle of the buildings. Elevated hallways, stairs, and ramps are rendered as a separate transit system within (and responding to) the massing. There are moments of acceleration, where nodes of circuitry, massing, and enclosure collapse into a coarse whole.

93

Delicately balanced to the point of falling or breaking, and flooded with line work, Prix's projects often have the sense they are about to move.

Busan Cinema Center, Busan, South Korea, 2012

94

The design of circuitry in this manner could be described as a way of both managing and curating speeds, showing and concealing them.

What is profound is how that circuitry allows one to navigate the upper recesses and secreted portions of the buildings as much as they serve to get one from point A to point B. These circuits foster roaming, exploration, and

Akron Art Museum, Akron, OH, USA, 2007

discovery in a manner that encourages one to engage ceilings, ceiling-walls or other elements intimately. Like reaching your hand out of the window while driving to feel the air, you glide and brush up against the building. This is compounded by the Möbius strip-like circulation geometries, which often disorient, reorient, bend, and rotate the visitor into a multitude of positions, dislocating the entry and losing one's position. The experience is as intimate and immersive as it is distant and spectacular, producing a texture of public or semi-public spaces and speeds that foster an immense potency for urban use. Blurriness or clouds have been a subject related to the work of Coop Himmelb(l)au. The overlapping of contour and profile lines, of structural hierarchies and member sizes, of differently tessellated structural geometries, of different cladding systems, ranging from reflective to matte—all always in gray—has an inescapably hazy affect. This articulation supports the desire to come into close contact with the building and get lost in it. Like grasping to feel rain, you do so because you cannot really see it; you need to touch it to sense its density and rhythm. To this extent, the rendition—the litany of raw, exposed details, of intersecting or overlapping cladding and structural systems—mutes what might otherwise be a tangible, legible, and clear speed; they veil and obfuscate it.

The title "The Possible Impossibility" might suggest that what was once impossible to the architect is now possible. In the context of Hong Kong, where the lecture was delivered, one might further conclude that this title means the impossible is now possible in China; a natural anticipation one might have reinforced by the fact that the lecture overlapped with the nearing completion of the Dalian International Conference Center (2012). However, in the context of this lecture series and the notion of speed, it is equally important to understand and identify the civic contribution of work like Prix's. Because of the dexterity of the building experience and prowess of curating structure, circulation, and cladding, there is a palpable cadence to the spaces that are publicly accessible. Even when his buildings do not necessarily include public spaces, you can see an effort to steal them from the adjacencies, tuck them in, cover them; making their boundaries blurred and as centripetal as they are centrifugal.

UFA Cinema Center, Dresden, Germany, 1998

In a 21st-century city like Hong Kong, where everyone and everything is moving as fast and efficiently as possible, one might conclude that the architectural antidote to the city would be to make a "slow" building. Yet Prix and his work with Himmelb(l)au promise that architects can use speed, manage it, design it, accelerate it, and slow it down to foster extended durations and a heightened attentiveness in the public realm. This sense of speed is evident in abundance in Prix's buildings. It is precisely those moments within his work—when all synapses are firing and one is in the moment, losing time, losing their position—that are so critical to cities and their continued vitality. If there is anything that might be "impossible," it is considering how to design that affect in a building and Prix is among a rare few who have made that impossibility possible.

IN_FORM

Form has been both a central tenet and an equally controversial concept anchored in the discipline of architecture. One could argue that form's primacy in Architecture (with a capital A) is the distinguishing factor between Vitruvius's *De Architectura* (30–50BCE), comprised of 10 books that are typologically centered and do not explicitly address "form," and Alberti's *De re aedificactoria* (1443–1452), also 10 books, which incite Platonic and Aristotelean concepts of "universal form" as a counterpoint and critique of *De Architectura*. In other words, the historical establishment of the discipline, its scholarly pursuit, and importance in the social, cultural, and philosophical realm not only situate form as an anchor in architecture discourse but also inextricably link form and typology, form and social politics, form and the sacred, form and philosophy; making the perceived, still lingering, and contemporaneously popular discursive antagonism between the formal and the informal, and between the formal and the social both amnesiac and problematic.

The intention of the following introductions is not so much to define form as it is to expose its varied meanings and open up the space between our disciplinary comfort or discomfort with form and its counterpart—the informal.

The debate between these two discourses, more recently seeded in the mid-20th century with the end of CIAM and the launch of Team 10, has implicit influence on our post-digital praxes and thinking today.

The question is whether these terms continue to reinscribe themselves in a somewhat binary, acrimonious manner —as they did in the late part of the 20th century, when "the formal" equaled an autonomous, unengaged, abstract and geometrically based practice, and "the informal" was positioned as an engaged, real, humanitarian, and programmatically based practice.

This dichotomy was further reduced to how architecture is formed versus how it is informed, as Jeffrey Kipnis sagely insinuated in his infamous essay in *Folding in Architecture* (1992).

Today, are there new ways of understanding form that might be productive to examine, jarring us out of a disciplinary and professional "holding pattern"? The following introductions highlight the contradictions and perhaps not-so-obvious aspects of each participant's work as it relates to form, seeking to cull out the richness of their contributions to this particular discursive strain.

Geometries transform into mediums, sociopolitical frames are enmeshed into formal processes, rituals inscribed, and interdisciplinary threads seeded; diffusing disciplinary oppositions between the formal and the informal.

Through this line of questioning, form could be understood as the antecedent to the object and therefore an undercurrent of the "object turn" in architecture discourse.

These introductions were written at a time that parallels the launch of Graham Harman's Object Oriented Ontology, or Triple O, and

its infiltration into architecture.
By implication, they allude to the
transformation of the debate between
form, the informal, and the object as
a pertinent triumvirate of subjects in
the discipline.

While objects and object-hood are
not explicitly foregrounded here,
the discourse surrounding questions
of the object—through the lens of
form—opens up its potential meanings
and value; something only possible
through these equally compelling
figure's work and thinking.

VECTORS, ARCS, AND TANGENTS

INTRODUCING
HANI RASHID

Architecture has a complex and insecure relationship with the term form. It is a term with a varied and rich history, one that is entrenched in politics and culture. Architectural form and the presumptions that it is stable, object-like, or even legible left the discipline over 50 years ago—yet this idea of form persists in many student's education today. For Hani Rashid and Lise Anne Couture form is anything but stable. It is saturated with imagery, part virtual and part real, forming and informing at the same

Clockwise from top: The ARC Museum, Daegu, Korea, 2012 / Moscow Contemporary Hermitage Museum, Moscow, Russia, 2021 / Steel Cloud, Los Angeles, CA, USA, 1988 / Beukenhof Auditorium and Crematorium, Schiedam, the Netherlands, 2012

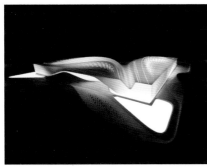

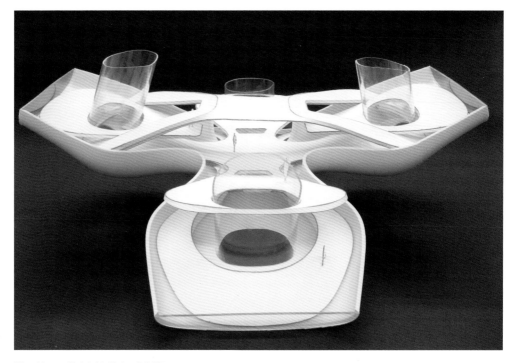

Wing House, Helsinki, Finland, 2011

time. Their acclaimed firm Asymptote is one of the few practices in the discipline to meticulously work through the problem of the virtuality of form today. Asymptote's work reflects an incredibly deep understanding of the potentials of form both in its geometrical aspects and its cultural affiliations. This understanding emerges out of a practice that has spent over 20 years trying to come to terms with how to work with one of the most rudimentary aspects of form: the line.

In its most classical sense, the line is that which divides interior from exterior, that which sets up boundaries. It is a fundamental part of what defines architectural form and its political associations. In the title of this evening's lecture, in the name of their firm (an asymptote is two converging lines that don't meet), and consistently in their projects, lines are always embedded within form. What distinguishes Asymptote's research on the line is the many

■ RASHID

Form is anything but stable. It is saturated with imagery, part virtual and part real, forming and informing at the same time.

ways in which lines are manifest within the work. Whether it is a projected line on the surface of a model, interior, or building; a wireframe exposed within the surface of a rendering; a crease within a building enclosure; or the thin void between masses, lines take on many different forms in Asymptote's architecture. To some extent, their work redefines the line and thus takes an innovative position on form and the politics of design. Instead of being stable, clear, and well-defined, Asymptote's architecture is caught in a state of "actualization," (2010) their projects are "scapes," (2004) in "flux" (2002) or "at the interval" (1995), as the titles of their four monographs infer.

The line may seem very basic to some designers, but as with much of architectural theory and practice, things are often not what they seem. The task of redefining line and subjugating its definition to new forms, requires intensive experimentation, risk-taking, and research; all of which are evident in Asymptote's work.

Even though they are building all around the world, they continue to participate in numerous exhibitions and design installations, most of them exhibited and collected by some of the world's leading arts institutions such as the Guggenheim, Centre Pompidou, and MoMA. Each of these—including their repeated participation in the Venice Architecture Biennale—is an opportunity to experiment with a broad range of media, technology, and materials. From the use of inflatable architecture, snow, and interactive technologies, to the production of virtual galleries and object-products saturated with information, their experimentation with the material of the line versus the "image" of the line shows an acute understanding and simultaneous questioning of what constitutes form.

The HydraPier Pavilion, Haarlemmermeer, the Netherlands, 2002

Asymptote is working at a significant range of scales, from product design to master plans, from pavilions to museums, ports, and towers. Their HydraPier Pavilion (2002) in the Netherlands—a building that demonstrates how two lines physically support, define, and articulate surfaces and mass—is at its center flooded with water. Sheen and reflection are materialized to produce

Their experimentation with the material of the line versus the "image" of the line shows an acute understanding and simultaneous questioning of what constitutes form.

■ RASHID

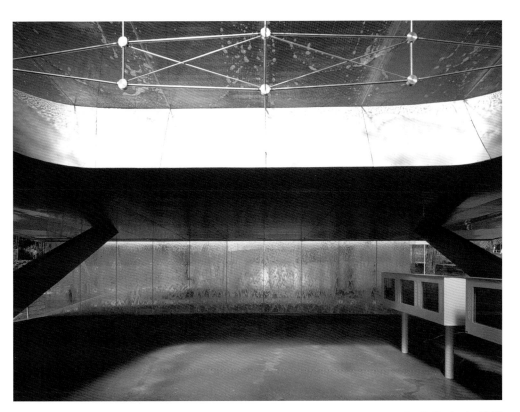

The HydraPier Pavilion, Haarlemmermeer, the Netherlands, 2002

a heightened sense of imagery, saturation, and depth. Animation is not something relegated to the design process but vital, integrated into the live experience and material fabric of the project. This simultaneous temporal dissolution, acceleration, and articulation of form is evident in many of their projects and at numerous scales. It is calibrated in the use of several media, such as light and water, as well as in their use of materials like resins, plastics, and glass.

Hani Rashid, who is joining us to present Asymptote's work this evening, has stood out as a leader and thinker in the discipline since Asymptote was launched on to the scene by winning first prize for the Los Angeles Gateway competition. Entitled Steel Cloud (1988), the project simultaneously showed

Rashid's roots at Cranbrook and exhibited the potential to separate himself from those roots. A delirious assemblage of lines floating above and absorbing the cityscape of Los Angeles, simply in title, one already sees their oxymoronic and multiplicitous "take" on form; it is both steel and cloud, line and vapor. Perhaps it was the graphic saturation of lines on top of lines or the display screens weaving text into its super structure that distinguished this project and made it so significant.

Whatever one might imagine as the many merits of that project, it was clear to critics, students, and fellow colleagues that Asymptote stumbled onto a provocative way of thinking about architecture. It was the beginning of a thesis about architecture where lines simultaneously materialize and dematerialize form. Perhaps these are some of the *Vectors, Arcs, and Tangents* Rashid will elaborate on this evening.

Please join me in welcoming Hani Rashid.

Top and bottom: Yas Marina and Hotel, Abu Dhabi, UAE, 2010

ELEGANT FORMATIONS

INTRODUCING
ALI RAHIM

From our lectures in this series, we have come to understand that form is not stable and that it is something that involves various processes. Contemporary Architecture Practice (CAP), the firm of Ali Rahim and Hina Jamelle, stands apart in the discourse of architecture because it debunks one of the fundamental tropes of form. Their work demonstrates how form must be understood not as the termination of a process, but as something that is both responding to and launching many different processes. In Rahim's words, this is "feedback" that occurs both in the process of design and once a project is actualized.

Top and bottom: IWI Orthodontics, Tokyo, Japan, 2010

Their work demonstrates how form must be understood not as the termination of a process, but as something that is both responding to and launching many different processes.

Architects tend to distinguish between "objects" and "fields." In the past 10 years, there have been articles and books written that suggest "architecture is moving from an object to a field." I would suggest that these types of distinctions imply a general trend away from form and toward the urban. The moral imperative underlying this strain of discourse is that "the field" is good and "the object" is bad. Furthermore, one might be persuaded to presume, through writings and critiques oriented in this manner, that a field is responsive or functional, and that the object and form are excessive or self-indulgent. To put it yet another way, one could conclude form is about the icon and not about the city or the site.

A distinguishing characteristic of CAP's work is that one does not see the separation of objects and fields. Not only in their unique methods of making renderings and drawing plans, sections, and diagrams but also in their final built work, fields are often enmeshed into and through a design object. By eroding the boundaries between methodological techniques that are often seen by designers as oppositional—take for example the mapping techniques of urbanism versus the precise geometrical and parametric techniques of architectural fabrication and interiors—CAP integrates the urban circulation, program, and site contours of each project as the progenitor of form. In so doing, their body of work forges a larger polemical assertion that contemporary architectural form is in fact a "formation." Formations are key to understanding their work because they are not only generated by processes but also "catalyze" processes, be it urban, material, or programmatic; as is implied by the title of Rahim's book *Catalytic Formations: Architecture and Digital Design* (Taylor & Francis, 2006). In this sense, one could understand

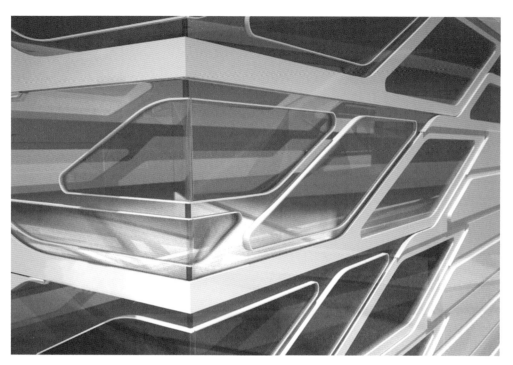

Chelsea Condominium Tower, New York, NY, USA

Rahim's work as being "in_formation." Now one might ask what does elegance (noted in this evening's lecture title and in Rahim and Jamelle's writing) have to do with this? Or what does elegance have to do with architecture? Elegance is a type of restrained beauty that suggests a certain level of simplicity. Insisting that the mere use of technology is not enough to ensure design ingenuity, Rahim and Jamelle have argued that architectural design must engage broader social, cultural, and aesthetic initiatives; otherwise it lacks value and limits discourse. While they are designers that continue to experiment with new digital tools in their design process, they also recognize that more information does not necessarily lead to better design. Admittedly, they are critical. They go so far as to note that more technology can, in fact, result in "bad" design and that the cultural and social awareness of certain aesthetic sensibilities, like elegance, are crucial for these technologies to have sustained value.

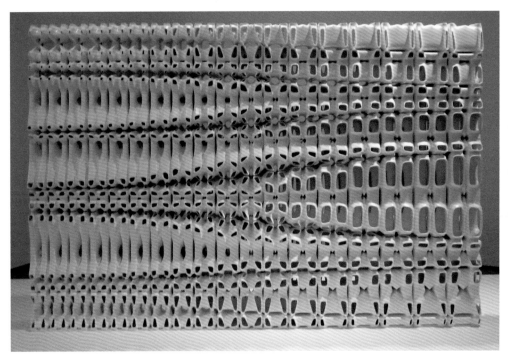

MoMA Home Delivery, New York, NY, USA, 2008

I suspect this criticality about technology is a particularly acute syndrome one becomes aware of when working with their concept of formations; largely because they are working the interior and the exterior, the urban and the detail at the same time. What I see as distinguishing elegance in their work is their ability to cull a minimum number of assembly strategies out of vast fields of code and geometry that works at more than one scale, with more than one material. Whether it is tweaking the contours of a site and threading them into a home to partition rooms for a fashion designer or generating a field of lines that transform mullions into stairs and shelves for a retail store in Shanghai, their work and renderings have a level of refinement that is extreme. From the coordination of air conditioning grilles to the thinness of mullions and the rippling optical refraction of glass, their work shows a deep commitment to "fineness."

Their body of work forges a larger polemical assertion that contemporary architectural form is in fact a "formation."

Rahim and his firm work at a range of scales, from designing furniture and lighting fixtures to high rises, libraries, houses, and exhibitions. Even at the scale of furniture or the prototype of a wall, a larger field of possible contours and information is apparent in the design process and how the design engages the actual surrounding space. Projects like the IWI Orthodontics Clinic (2010) showcase this potentiality through the versatile way in which a field of contour lines—some artificial lighting, some panel seams—extend from interior to exterior, becoming paver patterns and expansion joints. Mostly white on white, the design of the clinic is a hypnotic, embossed, three-dimensional texture that is constantly shifting your perception and understanding of the space. That texture extends onto the terrace producing a distinctly urban dimension which, not unlike Japanese landscapes, skilfully manipulates short and long views; it works to interiorize the surrounding urban fabric. It is uncanny how the project uses the simple and esoteric constraints of the project, like panel size, seams, and expansion joints, to transform what is otherwise a series of rooms into a larger fabric-field. It is both deeply interior and urban at the same time.

Rahim has been at the center of architectural discourse in the United States and Europe for the past 15 years because terms like "catalytic formations" and "elegance" are so adroit in redefining our basic understanding of the differences and similarities between form and processes.

He was not only the first of an emerging generation of digital designers to edit an issue of *AD*, but went on to edit three of their most seminal issues. Each reflecting his broader thesis with titles like "Contemporary Processes in Architecture" (2000), "Contemporary Techniques in Architecture" (2002), and "Elegance" (2007), his books bravely struck out to make political and social

CAP Offices, Shanghai, China

a number of technical processes that were otherwise left to the obsessions of architecture technophiles.

Rahim's enthusiasm about design and interest in articulating ways in which architects can "catalyze cultural advancements" speaks to his continued investment in architectural material, form, and its associated cultural values. It is also clear from his writing and work that he believes technology is part of what fuels design ingenuity. What sets his work apart is a deeper understanding of the relationship of how those technologies shift our understandings of form; it is both object and field, it is both the processes that generate and that act upon form once it is actualized. It is through this wrestling between "states of becoming" that one can understand his work as being in a perpetual state of "formation"—perhaps even "elegant." Please join me in welcoming Ali Rahim.

Samsung Residential Towers, Seoul, South Korea

UNDISCIPLINED DISCIPLINE

INTRODUCING
DONALD BATES

Digging into the etymological roots of "form" in previous lectures, we have come to observe that contemporary discourse surrounding form engages the word's origins in our discipline, entangling processes and fields, politics and culture as part of the repertoire of ways in which form can be understood. Donald Bates is one of the few architects able to articulate the ways in which his work deals with the schizophrenic and unclear disciplinary definitions of form. It is a topic that is as much disciplined as it is undisciplined, as this evening's lecture title might suggest.

Top and bottom: Federation Square, Melbourne, Australia, 2002

NGV Building, Federation Square, Melbourne, Australia, 2002

His design for Federation Square (2002) in Melbourne, which launched his now world-reputed, award-winning firm LAB architecture studio, is unique in many respects. The project is emblematic of how cities in the late 20th century tried to deal with issues of urban identity and city building. It is at once a collection of many diverse building typologies and a single project; it is a neighborhood and architectural icon at the same time; it is both a private commercial space and the site of political protest and celebration. In many respects, the project represents the heterotopic dream of numerous architectural theories.

■ BATES

Bates is one of the few architects able to articulate the ways in which his work deals with the schizophrenic and unclear disciplinary definitions of form; it is a topic that is as much disciplined as it is undisciplined.

With his partner Peter Davidson, Bates took on the challenge to develop an architecture that could balance the dexterous needs of the project against its requirement to produce a singular, civic image, identity, and coherence.

It is through this project that their understanding of form matured and took hold. The work of LAB postulates form not as an object, image, or even necessarily a process but as something that is at once drawing and building, coherent but not continuous. This concept sets their work apart from their peers. Unlike most building elevations, Federation Square is cloudy and appears randomized. During different times of the day and in different solar orientations portions are veiled, deep, and translucent, while in other locations they are thin, solid, and opaque. As Bates so elegantly phrases it, the project is a meditation on the "specific versus the generic, formally expansive versus constrained," a project that required an "interoperability" of "surface to form."

There is no doubt that the collection of buildings comprising Federation Square was designed by two people who are devoted to drawing and understand both its formal character and informal potential. Alluded to in exhibitions of their work, entitled Draw the Line and Lineage, not to mention Bates's repeated use of the word "grillage" as a descriptor of their projects, Federation Square is bound to the variegated architectural discourses on drawing and form. While LAB's mentors were part of a collection of thinkers who critiqued "The Plan" and while many of their peers were trying to reinvent how to design in section—both comfortable expressions of architecture with a capital A—LAB bravely took on the subject of the elevation; a subject not so comfortable to architects at that time. Elevation had a sort of taboo among designers in the

124

Bates has been consistent and persistent, rethinking the basics of drawing as something that not only generates form, but dissolves it.

1990s, who saw it as superficial and about the image. Venturian in its legacy, elevation was the last place one might find form; it was all sign.

Yet, LAB incredibly developed an architectural thesis that postulates how an elevation has spatial potential, how it can both delineate and be indeterminate; or as Bates puts it, how drawing can produce an "indeterminacy of delineation and still have a clear reading of space, event, or function."

Insisting that the elevation can both adapt to use, its context, and at the same time materialize and dematerialize form, is asking 500mm to 1,000mm of architecture to do a lot of work. Federation Square does precisely this and was only the beginning. The seed of a much larger body of conceptual ideas and technical innovations, LAB's work on double-thick facades, porous enclosures, rationalizing randomness, and conceiving ways in which a building can be spatially affected by its perimeter, "The Elevation" for Don and Peter is much more than an enclosure, surface, or facade, and certainly more than simply the delineation of form. It is both wireframe and solid. This is evident in the range of their projects, which test this body of ideas from China and Singapore to the United Arab Emirates, Saudi Arabia, and Lebanon, to the United Kingdom and Australia through an incredible portfolio of typologies, ranging from master plans to resorts, office towers, and cultural institutions.

Bates was a seminal teacher at the Architectural Association in the 1990s, the Founding Director of the Laboratory of Primary Studies in Architecture (LoPSiA), and taught at the Cooper Union in New York. He has been a recurrent voice in the discipline, has contributed to a wide variety of critical journals

ACMI Building, Federation Square, Melbourne, Australia, 2002

Federation Square, Melbourne, Australia, 2002

for over 20 years, has lectured and sat on reviews at over 95 schools, and is (now) both a professor and the chair of Architectural Design at University of Melbourne. Bates's teaching and writing are witness to the determination and distinguished manner in which he has pursued a rather complex and nuanced set of ideas about contemporary form.

Bates has been consistent and persistent, rethinking the basics of drawing as something that not only generates form, but dissolves it. He has ingeniously considered how drawing is something that is intrinsic to form, geometry, and

Top: south atrium, BMW Edge, Federation Square, Melbourne, Australia, 2002
Bottom: north atrium, Federation Square, Melbourne, Australia, 2002

BATES

the discipline, while also recognizing the necessity to embrace graphics, as means of moving beyond traditional notions of form and understanding what drawing is "after," what it is pursuing or projecting; as the seminal *AD* entitled "Architecture After Geometry" (1997), edited by Peter and Don, so aptly alluded to.

Don Bates is one of a few architects who continues to show the courage to take on challenging new ideas and give them sophistication. Evidenced in his projects and writing, one can see a willingness to struggle with and locate a space between unadulterated heterogeneity and extreme coherence. Perhaps what Bates is "after" is to position work on the fulcrum; precisely at the point where it is coherent and simultaneously incoherent, where form appears and at the same time it evaporates. This is perhaps a way of suggesting that being undisciplined within the discipline is more productive than being undisciplined outside the discipline.

Please join me in welcoming Don Bates.

Federation Square, Melbourne, Australia, 2002

THE RITUALS OF ARCHITECTURE

INTRODUCING
HERNÁN DÍAZ ALONSO

We have been learning through this series of lectures that much of the contemporary discourse on form counters our presumptions about it; namely that it is no longer an object, that it is certainly urban and political, and that it seems to have as much to do with representing architecture as it does the perception of completed architectural works. Many architects and historians regard form in unique and contrasting ways—a testament to both its dexterity and ambiguity.

Top and bottom: Pitch Black, MAK Centre Exhibition, Vienna, Austria, curated by Andreas Kristof, 2007

The work is about shifting the forms of architecture beyond building and embracing the architectural cinematic

Moral imperatives present in the discipline, such as the notion that urbanism is for the public and form is for the self-indulgent, are turned on their head in Hernán Díaz Alonso's work with his firm Xefirotarch. While his monograph, titled *Excessive* (2008), and the appearance of the work may lead one to think that his work is concerned with gratuitous form-making, I would like to suggest another reading: the work is about shifting the forms of architecture beyond building and embracing the architectural cinematic.

Díaz Alonso's work has a strong relationship with principles of urbanity that drive the production of cities. It can be argued that urbanity—as opposed to urbanism—is bound to fantasy and, more specifically, by a desire for cinematic experiences. Georgy Simmel's "blasé" and Walter Benjamin's "distracted" urban dwellers, underpin a significant proportion of 20th-century architecture discourse that was devoted to this endeavor. Among other architectural cinematics that emerge from this discourse on the city, the montage, the fade, the cut, and animation have all been used to visualize architectural form, as techniques to generate architectural form or to activate the perceptual apparatus of form through the mechanisms of elevators, ramps, and escalators. This resulted in speculative proposals by architects where cites move, where they are "delirious," or "play." Cities in this capacity are understood as acts and involve modes of performance that are often (in today's technophilic software driven educational system) overlooked or misunderstood as being either against form and for program or against design and for urbanism.

Díaz Alonso's work stands apart because it re-opens the question of the relationship between form and performance, which has "form" in the center of its very word. While many architects have been using film software to generate architectural form, most of these designers focus on performance

Sangre, SFMOMA, San Francisco, CA, USA, curated by Joe Rosa, 2006

in the quantitative sense; think parametrics. Contemporary architects tend to shy away from the symbolic or imagistic aspects of their work, keeping form abstract. Díaz Alonso embraces the quantitative and imagistic by couching both within the auspices of cinematic performance. Image, mood, sensation, and the temporal structures of sequence, narrative, and plot are all evident in the design of his projects and blatant in the way he describes and self-titles them. The work looks unquestionably grotesque and horrific. He projects an alternative discourse of form surrounding his work. There is a growing entourage of students he has taught, who are becoming the leaders in visualization and modeling.

Every chance he gets he publicly confesses his desire to be a film director. Perhaps most importantly, there is a clear thesis about the interactive manner in which the work is meant to be experienced, perceived, and used in the

DÍAZ ALONSO ■

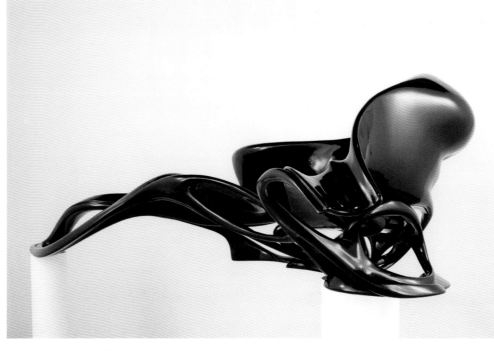

La Chaise Grotesque, 2011

city and by the city. An emerging and alternative discourse on performance, tethering it to the cinematics of urbanism, his projects are a performance of sorts.

Díaz Alonso's work is distinct from his peers, many of whom look at how populations of small parts aggregate together. Underlying the tendency among many of these designers is a sort of "design by inevitability." The processes that generate the work argue for it and argue for its appearances; "it is this way because of these processes." However, Díaz Alonso's work is definitively against legibility, it does not expose either the parts or the generative process.

Often mirrorized and sharpened to a point, the "thorny" tectonics and material sensibility of the work are astonishing. Instead of an architecture with clearly defined part-to-whole relationships, Díaz Alonso's "cells" (as he calls them)

La Chaise Grotesque, 2011

are often already assemblies comprised of both surfaces and lines, frames and enclosures, assemblies of two scales and often two or more materials. This allows them to have a certain promiscuity between structure and cladding, interior and exterior, circulatory path and structural frame. In each project, cells are woven together ("accumulated" as he phrases it) into a chiasma of circulation and potential programs with a range of spatial textures that oscillate between the very dense and the very sparse.

Mutation is an important theme in the work and clear in how each project's organization and tectonic are generated. Less obvious and more potent, however, is the mutation of his work in different contexts; which he has willingly undertaken and experimented with, unlike many of his peers. Díaz Alonso has used group exhibitions at some of the most prestigious institutions (MoMA in New York, SFMOMA in San Francisco, the Architectural Association

Díaz Alonso's work is definitively against legibility, it does not expose either the parts or the generative process.

in London, and the Art Institute of Chicago), as well as the Venice, Beijing, and Seville Biennales as a showcase to test these ideas; perhaps most evident in his solo exhibitions.

Rather than exhibiting the processes that derive architectural projects, Díaz Alonso uses these venues to engage the gallery goer and mutate the work. Entitled Emotional Rescue (2002), Sangre (2006), and Pitch Black (2007)— each familiar pop cultural titles from music and film here resituated in an unfamiliar gallery-based setting—the exhibitions are immersive and in your face. You do not stand back and ponder them; you are thrown into them and are encapsulated by a flurry of textures, finishes, and materials. It is difficult to distinguish if something is a model or a prototype, a piece of furniture or architecture. He shifts the medium of the gallery into something like a film, where the point is not to understand how the work was developed but to develop an emotional connection to the space.

Díaz Alonso won the highly-coveted MoMA PS1 Young Architects Program, a metro plaza competition in Kentucky, and received first prize or honorable mention in competitions in France, Korea, and Argentina. An urban plan intoxicatingly entitled Chlorophilia (2006), tableware called Mutant Manners (2002), a cell phone called Cell (2005-2006), and furniture with the title Chair Grotesque (2011), his wide range of projects use "The Excessive" to set up possible modes of interaction.

Neither an unadulterated open field framework nor a collection of completely closed figures, his projects often layer figure upon figure, producing orchestrated fields of porous massing. They literally take on a character-like

Top and bottom: MoMA PS1 Young Architects Program, New York, NY, USA, 2005

quality in their context. Be it someone's face, a table, the city, or the interior of a house, his projects have a vitality and life of their own.

Díaz Alonso is one of the most influential teachers right now and has developed an accomplished academic career in a relatively short time. His broad reaching academic influence reflects the fact that he not only embraces and experiments with contemporary media and technology, but most importantly that he does not foreground those technologies as the point of the work.

One can talk about the technical merits, bravado of process and technique, structural, urban, ecological, or even cinematic aspects of Díaz Alonso's work and teaching. However, that would be missing the point of this evening's lecture. Many of the codes, laws, and regulations that form society and our urban environment have symbolic underpinnings and are ritualistic in nature. Perhaps what he is trying to suggest in tonight's title is that the fantastical and symbolic acts that underpin architectural form are a way to understand both new modes of abstraction and new modes of performance at the same time. This may have less to do with the quantitative and process-driven ideas of performance that are popularized in the profession today and more to do with the ways in which the performance of form is vital to our imagination, to our individual character, and our daily practices. I look forward to finding out.

Please join me in welcoming Hernán Díaz Alonso.

Colon Theater, 2013

THE DIMENSIONS OF FLATNESS

INTRODUCING
TAKASHI MURAKAMI

Takashi Murakami is a superstar. His many different roles as artist, collaborator, curator, the president of Kaikai Kiki Co., product designer, animator, and writer are each undertaken with an equal ambition, devotion, aptitude, and thoughtfulness. He exploded onto the international scene with his exhibition *Superflat* (2001), which brought contemporary Japanese art culture and its associated subcultures to the world. In addition, Murakami's work has been shown in numerous international solo exhibitions. His work and persona continue to be equally seductive and

Reversed Double Helix, 2005

Gagosian New York installation views

provocative. He needs no introduction. His lecture needs no title. I will let him and his work speak for itself. Before doing so, however, I want to address two very good questions which came up several times while organizing this event: why Murakami's work would be of relevance to architecture students and how it relates to the theme In_Form. In other words, how can the person who coined the term Superflat—whose exhibition and work are arguing that the world is becoming more two-dimensional—be relevant in a discussion about architectural form, and what does the production of his artwork have to do with the production of architecture?

As we have seen throughout this series of lectures, form is not very clearly defined even within the discipline of architecture. In_Form is meant as much as a provocation as it is intended as a theme that is open-ended and elastic. From the three Bergs who defined American post-war art criticism to Brian

Self-Portrait of the Manifold Worries of a Manifoldly Distressed Artist, 2012

O'Doherty, Rosalind Krauss, and others who have discussed the expanded fields of fine art, there is a rich collaborative and critical history of exchange between painting, sculpture, installation design, and architecture that questions the very form and boundaries of each discipline. Murakami's work engages this continued debate.

From an architectural perspective, Murakami's work suggests a form of prototyping and iterative development that allows each different medium and iteration to become its own "project."

Of note is the play between forms of drawing and modeling, and how one might understand "context" as another method of Murakami's production of form. From sculpture to painting to graphics to animation to product design and to curation, Murakami's work takes many "forms." When most architects make drawings or models and exhibit their work, they are developing or showing a process. The shifts between two-dimensional modes of representation and three-dimensional production are, in the most typical cases, representations of one another; another way to cut a project, another scale to examine it. Even when architects embrace the use of video game and special effects software for animation, often those sequences are used to describe generative processes. To this extent, the multiple media architects use to design and exhibit work often remain confined to their representational role and are describing the generation of form; the representations do not "shift" forms between modes of representation.

What is both similar to architectural design processes and contemporary with regard to Murakami's work in the post-Warholian world of art, is that he develops his characters and figures in iterative series using a variety media. This mode of digital, mechanical, and analogue reproduction resonates with the ways in which contemporary architects work; using a hybrid of computer and analogue processes prototyping, testing, fabricating, and finally building a project. At first glance one may think the processes are the same, but the media is different—drawing versus painting, sculpture versus building, and so on. Or that these are not the similarities but the differences between "Art" and "Architecture."

Top: Gagosian New York installation views
Bottom: *727 DOB*, 2003

However, as Murakami so aptly notes in his *Superflat Manifesto*, and as much as there may be differences, there is also a flatness between these media that has eroded disciplinary boundaries. Murakami's studio uses many similar technologies one would find in architectural design studios. What sets Murakami's work apart is the way in which the effect and form of each medium is distinct; I would suggest it is extra-architectural. This is reflected both in the structure of Kaikai Kiki Co., where he interlaces practices once isolated and alien to one another, as much as it is reflected in his work.

In other words, a painting of his recurring alter ego character, Mr. DOB, is not a two-dimensional representation of a balloon sculpture containing similar characters. The painting has to encapsulate certain spatial illusions and formal sensibilities; the cute and the monstrous, the light and the deep. However, it must do so in a different way than a balloon installation showcasing the same character. The line work must be altered and colored differently to adapt to the perceptual weight of the balloons; their scale, their orientation, and their experiential sequence. The resultant sculptures produce similar sensations to the paintings but through different means. From an architectural vantage point, Murakami's work suggests a form of prototyping and development that allows each different medium and iteration to become its own "project." In other words, one could see each of Murakami's pieces as isolated instances as much as a series, as prototypes developed in 2D or 3D, interwoven not by their processes (which are wildly inconsistent from iteration to iteration) but by their perceptual consistencies.

In describing the *Murakami–Ego* show (2012), Murakami suggested that, "Taking architecture as an analogy, you could say that my paintings are like buildings. On the surface, they appear very light and flimsy, but they're actually made of very solid materials underneath. The depth is visual."

Murakami bravely embraces the illusive and the use of special effects in his work. Both invoke a moral agnosticism and both have been seen (in the most stereotypical and pejorative ways) as "formal" in the discipline of architecture. What is critical about Murakami's work is that he uses that contrast—between

146

Murakami—Ego, 2012

what is on the surface and what is behind it—as a means to engage our perceptions; working and reworking multiple "forms" of engagement.

These implications are perhaps even more evident in the brilliant way in which Murakami re-forms the context of his exhibitions by combining paintings with sculptures and working off of his surroundings in innovative and daring ways. His installations often combine large and small format paintings, placed directly on top of wallpaper or floor vinyl. They produce a backdrop for sculptural figures, which are often not located in isolation but also placed on top of one another, compounding the depth and layered perceptual effects. With mixtures of pieces from the same and from different periods and series, with related but not the same content, the installations invent a new context; one that is simultaneously the future and the past, fabricated and responsive. With his installations Murakami invokes a high degree of contrast within each

Murakami uses the contrast between what is on the surface and what is behind it as means to engage our perceptions.

piece, in relation to one another and against their surroundings. Yet within the dynamic political, historical, and formal differences comprising each of those pieces, there is a cohesion that is palpable and stimulating. This is perhaps most evident in the Versailles exhibition (2010), where he mutates the context of the palace into his own. While there are many shrewd and interesting similarities between the content of his sculptures and the content depicted in the various salons of Versailles, what is perhaps most unique is the way in which texture, luster, color, and sheen transform each room. Murakami's three-dimensional sculptures are holographically and illusively woven into their environment. Each piece makes use of materials and textures from another time with ulterior meanings, allowing us to inhabit Versailles in new and powerful ways.

Context is perhaps the anchor of Murakami's work, which situates it strongly within the architectural realm. Murakami's lesson might be summed up by his slogan for young (particularly Japanese) artists, "Figure out a way to produce your own context." From the mixture of traditional Japanese silvering and anime, to conflating the flatness of graphic space with the three-dimensional form of perspective space, Murakami is perpetually dislocating something from one context to another. Geopolitically, his work is similarly unstable. The influences of the contexts of Los Angeles, Paris, and London inflect the way his work is received in Tokyo, and vice versa. As he puts it, he is, "translating for both sides." By working both within traditional forms of making art and between those forms, he opens his work up to both new and existing contexts. Murakami's opening words for the original *Superflat Manifesto* were, "Greetings, You Are Alive." I am excited to be awakened. Please join me in welcoming Takashi Murakami.

Flower Matango, Versailles, France, 2001-06

PROJECT_ING

Over the course of their career, architects will have many projects, but their Project is something that changes with significantly less frequency, if at all. Unlike fine art or journalism, which are commentary-based forms of reportage and interpretation, architecture must project into future contexts, economies, and modes of inhabitation. It is a speculative practice and discipline, simultaneously opening up a wide array of formats for exploring one's work as much as it does require immense rigor and consistency of approach.

In the increasingly fast-paced and demanding environments of our profession and educational institutions, to what extent do architects have time to develop a Project? Furthermore, can we question the value and capacity of contemporary practice to include speculative formats of projecting, such as non-client-based books and drawings?

Whether it is Vitruvius's *On Architecture* (1st century BCE), Le Corbusier's *Toward a New Architecture* (1923), Rem Koolhaas's *Delirious New York* (1978), or Jesse Reiser's *Atlas of Novel Tectonics* (2006), the presumptive teleology of "projecting" in education and the profession is a priori. The École des Beaux-Arts Architectural Thesis, which persisted until the late 20th century in most architecture schools but has since diminished in presence, is a case in point: the thesis project developed as a student is threaded through an architect's professional career. Similarly, a book by an early-career architect, often containing speculative theories, serves as a theorem awaiting proof through later built work.

As the following introductions imply, this a priori mode of projecting contradicts our contemporary modality of forming a Project and projecting. One might even be able to go so far as to suggest that a priori thinking never has been architecture's strength.

This teleological narrative is more aligned with philosophies of science and other practicums that are not appropriate to the variegated necessities of architecture discourse and its profession.

It is abundantly clear that in today's multiple praxes of architecture, speculation is a necessity which comes in at least two forms; speculating into the future and into the past. Through the following introductions, one might begin to see built work as but one format of output that is galvanized as a vehicle to analyze and critique one's work, but not necessarily as proof of concept.

Each introduction encapsulates a different persona, identifying four ways of understanding and developing a Project.

What is at stake here is the question of whether having a Project remains useful, how it may have changed in recent years, and to what extent our contemporary condition fosters the exploration and projection of ideas surrounding the things we design. The following introductions, through the work of these four designers and thinkers, suggest that having a Project is important, but it may no longer be singular.

Today, projecting is a mixture of both a priori and post-facto modalities. Alleviating the architect from the necessity of having an a priori Project allows the exigencies of practice to inflect and mutate their work, as evidenced in all four of the following cases.

Beyond that, it ratifies circular thinking, reflection, and a commitment to learning from one's work, as opposed to seeing projects, especially built work, as benchmarks along a trajectory that continues in a forward, uni-directional manner.

Most importantly, this collection of introductions opens up the prospect that a Project may have differing appearances and formats of output. It is not as singular as it has been historically suggested or manifest and yet is no less rigorous or impactful.

In the media-laden world of the 21st century, where one has the opportunity to engage a multitude of audiences, it is perhaps more important than ever to project and to consider how those multiplicitous formats of architectural projection can be engaged in impactful ways.

COSMOPOLITAN FIELD: THE ARTIFICIAL LOCAL

INTRODUCING
JESSE REISER

The title of this lecture, on the occasion of the publication of *O-14 Projection and Reception* (2012), is a testament to and reflection of the dexterity of the work of RUR and the thinking of Jesse Reiser and his partner Nanako Umemoto; who comprises the critical "U" in the palindromic RUR. While the built work of RUR has tremendous tectonic richness and the drawings and representations of their work serve as speculations as much as codifications of that work, it is perhaps through their books that we see their most ardent capacities for projection.

Clockwise from top left: Taipei Pop Music Center interior and exterior, Taipei, Taiwan, 2020 / O-14, Dubai, UAE, 2012 / Kaohsiung Port and Cruise Service Center, Kaohsiung, Taiwan, 2017

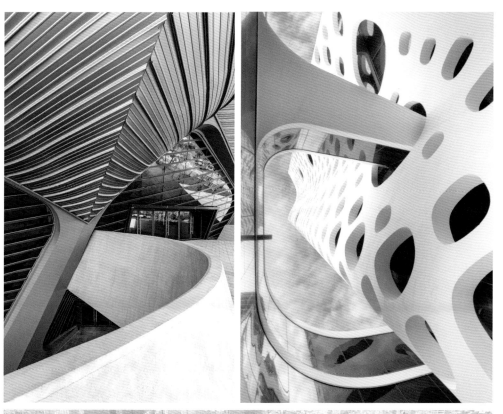

What is inherently impactful about their books; starting with *Atlas of Novel Tectonics* (2006) through *O-14*, and now with *Projects and their Consequences* (2019), is RUR's thoughtful and tight relationship between the words and the work. In all three books, the mood encapsulates an unapologetically post-facto theorization of design work while at the same time recognizing that the writing, theorization, and reflection upon the works each book collects is an act of projecting itself; looking backward and forward in an immensely productive way.

This use of writing and the related conception of the architect's book, forming the praxes of Reiser, Umemoto, and Reiser, are indeed as rare as the tripartite, multigenerational composition of their collaboration, which includes Debora Reiser, a lesser-known, mid-century canon in her own right. Architects and architecture have a complicated and storied history in their relationship to writing or, more specifically, the production of books. Common among that history is an assumption that the book often establishes the context and comes first, or alternatively, that it is an autonomous project from built work. Meaning, building is either the second act and a representation of theories originated in the tome or that the book is The Architecture, resulting in work/words/images without buildings.

Both literary trajectories have been lauded as much as criticized and continue to form the mainstream of educational pedagogy in most graduate schools of architecture, where writing and theorizing the work is among the most articulated attributes that distinguishes a masters or professional degree from an undergraduate degree.

What is not so commonly discussed in schools and has often been pejoratively dished off as disingenuous, is the act of reading and theorizing the work after it is built. Using the work as a platform for speculation has an air of immorality, retaining an almost religious alignment with the thinking that the idea comes first. Yet, this rare and somewhat counter-intuitive approach is precisely the space that Reiser and his "family" of collaborators precariously and bravely occupies in these books.

Reiser + Umemoto, Projects and Their Consequences, Princeton Architectural Press, 2019

O-14 (perhaps more so than *Atlas*) is unorthodox in that it recognizes the necessity of making books as a format of practice—part of the required, iterative circularities and refinements of doing sophisticated design work. Where *Atlas* may fall more into the a priori modality of writing, the "theorizing and then building" framework, *O-14* amplifies the latent post-facto themes within *Atlas* and puts them front and center. It is clearly both reflective and projective. To this extent, the book serves as a kind of "mid-term" for the building, using it as a springboard to cultivate and develop onward techniques and theories while also identifying past failures and trajectories that may become obsolete within future work.

Taipei Pop Music Center, Taipei, Taiwan, 2020

The content of the book and the title of the lecture reinforce this circular idea of projecting and identify it as an underlying strength of RUR's work over the years. While their practice and projects are strongly rooted in "context," they do not purvey a prevailing understanding of architectural context. One part disciplinary, one part technical, one part site, and one part environment, the "contexts" for RUR are not merely the surroundings, adjacencies, or existing cultures and physical conditions. They are "live" and projective. Buildings affect their surroundings, harness their optical reflectance, and animate the horizon.

Refusing to capitulate to entrenched understandings of context, work like Kaohsiung Port and Cruise Service Center (2010), O-14 (2006), and Taipei Pop Music Center (2010) vibrates in an uncomfortable, slightly preternatural (yet

O-14, Dubai, UAE, 2012

Through its qualities, the work activates a cosmopolitan field and sees the local as something to cultivate, harness, to make; it is artificial.

grounded) network of relationships. While each project might take cues from a conventional understanding of context that resonates with their surroundings via scale, texture, and materials, each also evokes acontextual strategies that augment their character; the building becomes a screen or has the qualities of an apparition. In many ways RUR's work is not local. Certainly, there are limited immediate associations with the surroundings. Yet through the artifice of the building and through the recognition that the surroundings are by implication cosmopolitan (entwining local and non-local agencies and networks), the buildings establish a vivid presence; more often than not re-originating and "flipping" their surroundings. In other words, where most buildings appear to be the most recent addition to the skyline or harbor's edge, theirs often leave an impression of having been there before anything else.

While I could speak at length about their overt and often geeky obsessions with the finitudes of architecture, ranging from their interests in the geodesic to laminar flows, it is in fact the longer arc of the projects that is the most pertinent to this series of lectures. The talk Reiser delivered advocates for a format of projecting that is anything but linear and futuristic. It embraces reflection, the theoretical distortion and the creative realignment of discourse networks as a means of finding dynamic and evolving value in completed projects.

Furthermore, it is through the space of the post-facto that RUR has discovered and cultivated an invaluable take on what is otherwise presumed to be known or understood: the subject of architectural context. Through its qualities, the work (and its associated theories) activates a cosmopolitan field and sees the local as something to cultivate, harness, to make; it is artificial.

Taipei Pop Music Center, Taipei, Taiwan, 2020

In a city striving to identify its geopolitics and with a questionable history of creative culture, Reiser brought to HKU the necessity for a new kind of critical thinking that would allow young designers to engage a context and city that might otherwise seem formulaic, overwrought, and impenetrable. As a distinguished professor, an accomplished architect, and someone who has been at the forefront of the discipline for decades, it is telling that Reiser and RUR are only now finding the voice to raise these types of questions and lay down their observations about their own creations. Others may see this as odd, they may opine that critics theorize the work after it is complete and may not see the value in reflecting so deeply on one's own designs that are built and completed; or worse yet, see it as narcissistic. I would argue otherwise. Reiser's will to publicly and theoretically explore his work is invaluable and a fable for younger generations to be attentive to. An insatiable mind and forbidding design talent, it was with great pleasure that we were able to welcome Jesse Reiser to offer his thoughts on Project_ing with our students.

ARCHITECTURE. POSSIBLE HERE?

INTRODUCING
TOYO ITO

What is Toyo Ito's Project with a capital P? What makes his method of "projecting" distinguishable from other contemporary masters? Ito is a challenging architect to pin down. Journalists have written extensively about the chameleonesque qualities of his portfolio of work and his seemingly shifting set of interests. Over the span of his career, the work does not have an explicit formal consistency. There is a veritable enthusiasm for exploring various interactive mediums such as wind,

Clockwise from top left: Za-Koenji Public Theatre, Tokyo, Japan, 2009 / Minna no Mori, Gifu, Japan, 2015 / Serpentine Gallery Pavilion, London, England, 2002 / National Taichung Theater, Taichung City, Taiwan, 2016

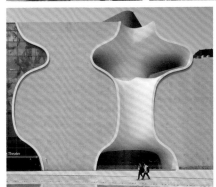

National Taiwan University Library, Taipei, Taiwan, 2013

light, sound, and structure; exacerbating the difficulty of stereotyping or summarizing his interests. While the materiality of lightweight materials is often associated with his practice as something unique, one could easily couch the aesthetic expression of "lightness" within a broader cultural framework by noting that this design sensibility (one that embraces entropy and delicacy) is prevalent and distinct to the philosophical, spiritual, and aesthetic discourses underpinning Japanese design—making those interests not so distinctive.

While we might all be able to recognize and appreciate the sensitivities with which each project draws from its variegated contexts and the uncommon free will of a talented architect to allow those contexts to influence the appearance of each project, scrutinizing Ito's work based on its appearance is probably the first misstep. What is clear is that his work is mysterious. It has a range of duration which shifts between the flatness and rapidity of image culture and

ITO

What is clear is that his work is mysterious. It has a range of duration which shifts between the flatness and rapidity of image culture to the messiness, depth, and thickness of material culture.

the messiness, depth, and thickness of material culture. We are drawn into it and want to explore it. There is a consistently palpable design of experience across multiple works. Perhaps this is a more suitable line of inquiry with regard to Ito's work; a trajectory that questions the extent to which the design of that "live experience" is shaped by a larger Project.

My own speculation on Ito stems directly from his early and current work with mediums. Though often invisible, mediums are perhaps one of the most consistent subjects of his work. Yet, he does not treat them in an essentializing manner (advocating for one medium as a "truth," as Kahn did with light) nor does he confine them to a limited set. The mediums he works with may seemingly randomly shift from wind to artificial light to structure to glass, steel, or wood. What is evident is his expertise in tinkering with mediums. There is a distinct inter-dimensionality to his work that is both exceptional and rare. There is a devotion to working with the intangible as something that drives and orchestrates the obvious, the visible. This combination of factors and the inconsistencies within the appearance of his work may be at the root of why Ito did not receive a Pritzker Architecture Prize until he was 71—in 2013, the same year as this lecture took place at HKU—because, one cannot so easily decipher the Project. Yet, I would argue that his Project is perhaps among the most pertinent to current and future generations of designers; outranking its importance among other Pritzker laureates.

The lecture at HKU came at a time when Ito was reflecting upon the cultural relevance of his work—its communal value and its impact—in a post-

Fukushima Japan. There was an overt turn toward the vernacular, to include the use of rough, non-planar wood, and to move away from the white washed, refined look familiar in previous projects. One has to recognize that to make an abrupt shift and to challenge one's own assumptions and skills is rare in the history of architecture. It is more common to set cruise control, ride out what you started and monetize it. This is not the case with Ito.

However, I would suggest that while there have been some distinct shifts in his career there remains a thread. Energies—seismic, catenary, luminous or pneumatic—pulse through and are reshaped by Ito's architecture. There is a clear idea about using dimensions, shifting them, producing textures of them, at different rates and speeds that persists in the work. In other words, there is a distinctly designed aspect to the live experience in his buildings that does not allow any one time or space to settle. One is often interacting in multiple times and spaces, and between the dimensions of the mediums he uses. Sometimes this is as simple as shifts from two dimensions to three dimensions, from super flat to thick, from matte to reflective. Mediums are often choreographed to heighten the differences between inside and outside, interiority and exteriority. In other projects we may see the use of less conventional, ulterior mediums—the interaction of wind and air, sound and light, color and line work.

While it may not be immediately apparent, one might correlate this notion of duration, sustained engagement, shifting of dimensionalities to intensive psychological experiences, where we lose time; flow experiences—like surfing or skiing—that typically put us into an intensified interaction with nature.

There is a distinct inter-dimensionality to his work that is both exceptional and rare. There is a devotion to working with the intangible as something that drives and orchestrates the obvious, the visible.

170

Sendai Mediatheque, Sendai-shi, Japan, 2001

Ito's precise and rigorous understanding of finishes, materials, structure, air, artificial light, color (and so on), their textures and how they interact is ultimately mediatric. The effect, as he designs it, leads to less of a "natural experience" than one that is a highly restrained "wildness." Subtle yet loud, quiet yet entrancing, it is clear why an architect who so deeply understands the use of media and its impact on live experience might have a book entitled, *Tarzans in the Media Forest* (2011) or a building based on media that is as material as it is ephemeral, such as the Sendai Mediatheque (2001).

This is a Project indeed, and perhaps a pioneering project—one that moves beyond the obvious, beyond what things look like and into how we interact with them—liberating the designer from a strict set of either formal or material configurations that define their many praxes.

At a time when it is critical for architects to understand how to use media (as opposed to avoid it) and discussions of discourse following the digital turn are openly being debated, the work and Project of Ito stands out as a beacon for future generations to consider as they engage the natures, environments, and contexts surrounding them.

To this extent one might be able to ask, where is architecture possible in a world saturated with mediums; a world wrought with dimensions we engage by the second, but which are not designed or considered? Or might we reverse that question and ask: Is architecture possible within this current cultural moment—here and now? The title of Ito's lecture suggests a prescience, a concern with the here and (if we extend this to include "the now") with live experience. Perhaps his work and larger Project could be seen as a guide for how we engage the here and now by embracing (rather than denying) the many media that comprise the cacophony of environments, that immerse the contemporary urban subject and which encourage us to see technology as something in parallel with nature and as another possible medium; as opposed to understanding those technologies as counter to nature. Ito's work on projecting is not obvious but is perhaps among the most important, making his work and thinking about the subject essential for its innovative and transformative capacities; relevant to architecture, possible here, today and in the near future.

Top and bottom: Tama Art University Library, Tokyo, Japan, 2007

THE FUGITIVE STATE OF ARCHITECTURE

INTRODUCING
NEIL DENARI

There are several very different ways in which architects "project." Some may use found materials, others may mix two- and three-dimensional techniques, while others may consider how to re-think "the model." To this extent, projecting is the act of conceptualizing the tools that produce the work as much as it is anticipating the effects and impact of the work on others; putting the psychoanalytical "-ing" in projecting. Projecting might be regarded by some as a thing that architects do when they have spare time and they are not too busy meeting contradictory, client-driven project briefs or juggling compounded deadlines. Or it might be regarded

HL23, New York, NY, USA, 2012

HL23, New York, NY, USA, 2012

as that which is relegated to academic endeavors, not part of the "core" of the necessities of the practice and profession. There are few architects who have been brave or smart enough to stitch the act of projecting together with a vibrant commercial practice; one that is driven by the speed and flows of contemporary commerce and media while balancing those forces with an air of self-critical reflection and forecasting. Neil Denari is one of those architects; a truly rare species among us.

Denari's work simultaneously and unapologetically engages architecture with the high-speed techniques of commercial media and culture. Even today, we somehow still find discourse espousing a moral agnosticism that divides projection from action. In some circles, acts of projection remain dangerously equated with a counter-cultural agenda; heralding slowness, permanence, or timelessness as the modus operandi for the 21st century. This type of thinking builds an ethos of architecture against media, architecture against commerce. As Denari so bluntly implies in his lecture title, this can relegate architectural discourse to a "fugitive state"; convicting it of crimes it never committed, reinforcing its detachment from the high-speed image-saturated world around it.

Denari, however, is no fugitive in these parallel worlds of architecture—the worlds of the practical and the projective architect, their potential commerce, their parallel praxes, methods, and consumer-driven visual culture. He is recognized as among the first contemporary designers to explicitly embed multiple practices of "design" into architecture. From automotive and product design to graphic design, this embeddedness manifests itself throughout his work. Often resembling mass produced products and aeronautical assemblies, Denari is the only architect I know whose resume includes an internship designing helicopters.

Using a patina of blues, greens, yellows, and, more recently, fuchsias and reds, Denari's work seems to possess the lightness of a mediated surface combined with the substance and material of architecture. For example, signage is not solely "applied" to Denari's architecture with Venturian purism. Text becomes the instigator of architectural surfaces that penetrate storefronts, that are enmeshed with the panelization of metallic masses, are integrated

Denari's work simultaneously and unapologetically engages architecture with the high-speed techniques of commercial media and culture.

MUFG Nagoya. Nagoya, Japan, 2006

with perforated building enclosures, and are formed into abstract calligraphy-like structures. There are uncanny moments in projects like HL23 (2009) where the pattern fritted on the glass is conflated with the steel bracing. The boundary where two-dimensional graphic design stops and architectural design begins is often unclear in Denari's work.

While he meticulously oversees every detail of his projects to an almost geek-like extreme, it is not for detail's sake. It is often because the sinuous and substantial surfaces of Denari's architecture are not paraded for geometry's sake alone. How these architectural surfaces embed media into their very fabric necessitates a degree of obsession and hint at how their design is both projective and tectonic.

Alan - Voo House Ph 1, Los Angeles, CA, USA, 2007

How Denari has been able to pay so much attention to his Project as well his many projects astounds me. His willingness to use architecture as a "medium of culture" is evident in his range of project types, many collaborations, and the numerous awards NMDA has received. NMDA has designed projects in Japan, Taiwan, the United States, Russia, China, and Slovenia. They have designed projects at many scales, from small residential additions to high rises, from commercial projects to institutional and civic projects, and have worked on numerous competitions including the Keelung Port Competition (2012) in Taiwan for which they took first prize.

While many of these works demonstrate how certain ideas are projected, their seeds are borne in exhibitions, installations, or in some cases his drawings. Interrupted Projections (1996), an acclaimed installation in Tokyo, took tropes of geometry (like Interrupted Goode Homolosine projection, typically used to spatialize and unfold the globe) and transposed ideas from one culture into another: from cartography into architecture. Misusing this system of mapping and folding to "lapel" and bend a blue-ish-green surface into a mass, Denari discretely tattooed logos, maps, screens, and CMYK symbols on the architecture in the installation. The experience is as if one is literally on the page of a book. The design produces a vivid scale inversion. Like Lewis Carroll's book *Alice In Wonderland* (1865), Denari's installation transforms information, galvanizes acts of reading into live content, and enmeshes them into a surface wrapping around, underneath, and above you; information gathering becomes haptic. This association of cultures, shifts of scale and practices is further heightened in the accompanying book (of the same title name and published by TOTO), which is one part graphic fodder, one part polemic, one part comic book, and one part design manual with logos designed for each project and dimensions literally projected out of buildings, as if the coding for construction was transformed into artifacts and built.

180

This work is compelling to say the least. It has captivated the attention of numerous students and peers world-wide. Yet Denari never dared indicate that somehow this is art, even fine art, or that the work is somehow against the flows of mainstream culture. In each of his installations and exhibitions, the work is always couched in a culture of consumerism and speed. Exhibitions like "The Artless Drawing" (2010) suggest this intent implicitly, if not explicitly. The title seems to buck directly up against the architectural "sketch" by suggesting that the "hand" is no longer present, but that the mechanisms of design are what gives something its "soul." Denari's early drawings (proto-digital, handmade, with double sided Mylar, using dot matrices of pre-printed, sticky-back Zipatone and stencilled letters) are immersive, hypnotic, and dense with design. The raw mechanical projection is their seduction.

Top: Interrupted Projects, Gallery Ma, Tokyo, Japan, 1996
Bottom: The Artless Drawing, UCLA, Los Angeles, CA, USA, curated by Sylvia Lavin, 2010

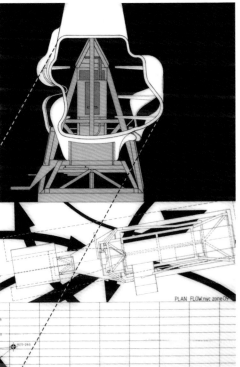

PLAN_FLOW.nyc zone09

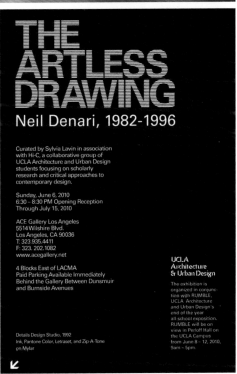

THE ARTLESS DRAWING

Neil Denari, 1982-1996

Curated by Sylvia Lavin in association with Hi-C, a collaborative group of UCLA Architecture and Urban Design students focusing on scholarly research and critical approaches to contemporary design.

Sunday, June 6, 2010
6:30 – 8:30 PM Opening Reception
Through July 15, 2010

ACE Gallery Los Angeles
5514 Wilshire Blvd.
Los Angeles, CA 90036
T: 323.935.4411
F: 323. 202.1082
www.acegallery.net

4 Blocks East of LACMA
Paid Parking Available Immediately
Behind the Gallery Between Dunsmuir
and Burnside Avenues

UCLA Architecture & Urban Design

The exhibition is organized in conjunction with RUMBLE, UCLA Architecture and Urban Design's end of the year all-school exposition. RUMBLE will be on view in Perloff Hall on the UCLA Campus from June 8 - 12, 2010, 9am – 5pm.

Details Design Studio, 1992
Ink, Pantone Color, Letraset, and Zip-A-Tone on Mylar

Sotoak Pavilion, El Paso, TX, USA, 2020

While Denari has engaged commercial practice full-heartedly, he has also earned a deep respect within the discipline. As the director of SCI-Arc, Denari was partly responsible for the shift of intelligentsia from the East Coast to the West Coast in the late 1990s. In Los Angeles, he started to see an emerging, projective, potential rejuvenation in the culture of the city and in what was an institution becoming a caricature of itself; where he seismically shifted SCI-Arc's culture to afford its current repute. His hugely popular monograph *Gyroscopic Horizons* (1999) encapsulates Denari's wit and sharpness as a designer who thinks about his work. The title invokes both the instability of a motion-based device, the gyroscope, and the classic architectural device of perspective, the horizon. This monograph is as highly visual and precisely textual, as it is easy and difficult in content. It pulls together themes bound to the discourse of the East Coast with trends and cultures of the West

Coast. It is this talent to associate cultures, manipulate media, and project architecturally that led Denari to the forefront of the discipline, taking the helm of SCI-Arc and now as a professor at the UCLA Department of Architecture.

I consider Neil a good friend and someone whom I have looked up to with enormous respect. There are very few architects with his kind of intelligence and willingness to continue to learn, who are also eager and willing to share, debate, and exchange ideas. Denari's work reflects this thoughtfulness and openness. He has forged collaborations with numerous design firms and seems to always be looking, seeking, and teasing architectural potential out of extra-disciplinary cultures and media. His opening to *Interrupted Projections* (1996) reads, "This book is a manual of ambivalence: that it proposes, in a world of never ending desires for the pleasure of newness, more images, more spaces, more icons, more words, Duo-tone Soul, Retinal Burn, Infographical Calm, these are the fluxual aesthetics of the contemporary landscape."

It seems to me these are humane desires from which contemporary architects cannot hide or retreat. Perhaps this means we should no longer feel like fugitives? Let's see. Please welcome Neil Denari.

183

SUPER

INTRODUCING
SARAH WHITING

We have had a wide array of voices in this lecture series. However, none of them so directly address the issue of projection and its importance in the discipline as Sarah Whiting. What distinguishes Whiting's voice on this subject is her ability to cast architectural projection as what some might call a "post-critical" endeavor; one which does not overthrow "the critical" but builds upon it, transforms it, and imbues it with distinctive agency within our many praxes as architects.

While she has numerous accomplishments in the field, it is writing that distinguishes Whiting among other thinkers and designers in the discipline. Her writing on projection is crucial in this respect. In numerous articles,

Select publications by Sarah Whiting

tracking a host of different subjects ranging from "the diagram" to "the super block," her work moves the discipline beyond modernism and postmodernism.

She is able to untangle age-old arguments about criticality versus style. She has an uncanny ability to thrust architecture onto a geopolitical stage, where the particularities of architecture form (and inform) their immediate political circumstances. At the core of this talent is Whiting's implication that projecting is a counterpart to the discipline's tradition of criticality. Whiting's projective architecture, while thoughtful and self-aware, is not about autonomous, abstract intellection. Whiting seems more interested in what architecture can do than how it is done, with a keen interest in how architecture and its projective capacities can "foreground force and effect."

She has an uncanny ability to thrust architecture onto a geopolitical stage, where the particularities of architecture form (and inform) their immediate political circumstances.

Counterintuitive in nature, her writings often upend our assumptions about their subject. In her article written with Robert Somol, "Notes around the Doppler Effect and other Moods of Modernism" (*Perspecta*, 2002), she spells out that while projective architecture "focuses upon the effects and exchanges of architecture's inherent multiplicities," it is not about legitimating architecture through interdisciplinarity or about architects literally becoming civil politicians. Rather than becoming less definitive, she suggests that projective architecture in fact re-asserts and redefines itself through its expertise "in relation to other disciplines," not by solely critiquing them.

Specific examples of her own ability to assert this disciplinary expertise are her articles on "the superblock." Examining a specific set of blocks in southern Chicago, Whiting has postulated new ways of reconsidering the superblock and the politics surrounding it. She turned what was deemed as a major protagonist in the death of American urbanism into a possible source of inspiration. Discussing Mies van der Rohe's canonical IIT campus plan as "bas-relief urbanism" and referring to SOM's Lake Meadows superblock as having an "urban thickness" that combines "slenderness and magnitude," Whiting adroitly expounds upon the elasticity and delicacy of the superblock— something historically characterized as crude and impenetrable.

She gives these projects distinct material sensibilities and registers their esoteric architectural moods. She simultaneously unpacks each project's effectiveness in Chicago politics through a specificity of design, while also culling out the intricacies of how the Chicago superblock impacts larger national trends and political initiatives. The value of such work is evident in both the critical reviews of her essay (which stood out among a blitz of related

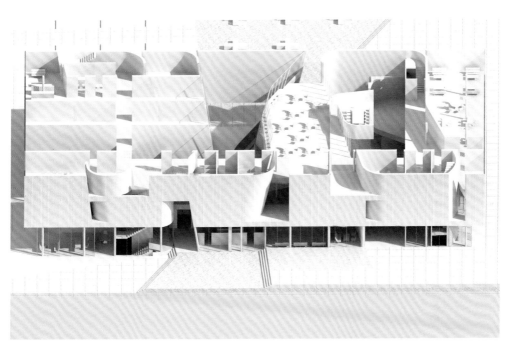

IntraCenter, Lexington, KY, USA, 2016

works about Mies) and the extent to which it was lauded and supported by key stakeholders in the profession.

Whiting founded, edited, and contributed to a journal called *Fetish*. Initiated with colleagues Stan Allen, Greg Lynn, and Ed Mitchell, *Fetish* tapped into and scrutinized the "sexuality and space" hype subsuming Princeton University's architecture school in the early 1990s. With some of the same cast of characters and in a similar role, Whiting went on to be a major contributor and the Reviews Editor at *Assemblage*—a journal that was already listing toward the post-critical. In contrast to its predecessor, the journal *Oppositions*, *Assemblage* was an effort to mix together ideas that were otherwise in dialectical opposition. It did so not by pitting manifesto against manifesto (as *Oppositions* did) but by mixing design projects with critical essays, forming a coarse assemblage of the types of media in each issue and spanning key subjects.

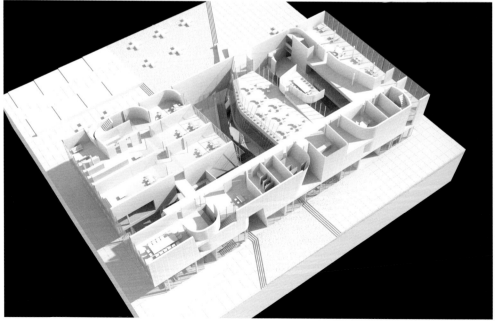

WHITING

Her work as both an editor and contributor stands distinctly apart from other journals (past and present) in its impact on discourse. She has contributed regularly to major theoretical journals, including *Any* and *Log*, where her articles continue to rough up the discipline and provoke new ideas. At the same time, her articles have appeared in mainstream outlets like the *New York Times* and *Wired* magazine. Her recent editorial project, as entertaining as it is incisive, is a series of short books called *POINT: Essays on Architecture*, which resituates discourse somewhere between "the pithy polemic and the heavily footnoted tome," by publishing long essays that construct a single point.

With seemingly no fear, Whiting has repeatedly taken on difficult, ambiguous, stereotypical, and poorly constructed subjects in architecture with an air of coolness and sheer intelligence. The clarity she brings to these subjects and the ferocity with which she affronts them are indicative of her accomplished academic career.

The kind of writing Whiting undertakes could only manifest from someone who is directly and intimately involved with design. She makes no excuses for architecture other than the design itself. In my opinion, this blunt attitude is partly formed out of her continued and active participation in the firm WW; which she co-founded with her partner Ron Witte in 1999. Their work and projects focus on a reinvigorated interest in figuration. Using what they call "two and a half dimensional" techniques and investigating material effects like "sheen," the conceptual territory and projective capacities of their work seems to hover just above the surface. Whiting's direct involvement in the Golden House and their winning competition entry for the San Jose State University Art Museum seem to reinscribe the cyclical implications of her projective architecture on their practice.

I cannot tell you how important it is to have someone like this in the discipline, nor can I over-emphasize the extent to which her work deserves immense

Top: Golden House, Princeton, NJ, USA
Bottom: IntraCenter, Lexington, KY, USA, 2016

Whiting has repeatedly taken on difficult, ambiguous, stereotypical, and poorly constructed subjects in architecture with an air of coolness and sheer intelligence.

respect. For example, Whiting's ability to break down canons like Manfredo Tafuri and Colin Rowe reflects a courage and talent rarely witnessed in architecture discourse; historically and today. She has gone so far as to suggest that Tafuri was a formalist and Rowe an astute politician; flipping the mainstream reception and histories of either figure's work upside down. What is so important about this inversion is that it overcomes the "politics versus form" argument; a divisive framing of discourse so often lauded (and stereotyped) by architects and historians alike.

Her project in some sense is to Project, to go beyond what is obvious and imbue subjects with a potential future. This is super; it is super interesting, super pointed, and super relevant.

Please join me in welcoming Sarah Whiting.

Golden House, Princeton, NJ, USA

RELATED TEXTS

Donald Bates:

Bates, Donald and Peter Davidson. "After Geometry," *Architectural Design* 67, No.5/6 (May–June 1997).

Kipnis, Jeffrey. *Perfect Acts of Architecture*. New York: The Museum of Modern Art, 2002.

Andrew Bromberg:

Bromberg, Andrew. *New Architecture in the Emerging World: Projects by Andrew Bromberg, Aedas*. London: Thames & Hudson, 2011.

Bromberg, Andrew. *Architecture and Sensuality*. San Francisco: ORO Editions, 2007.

Kipnis, Jeffrey, "Towards a New Architecture," *Architectural Design*, 1993.

Yung Ho Chang:

Bolchover, Joshua, Christine Lange, and John Lin, eds. *Homecoming: Contextualizing, Materializing, and Practicing the Rural in China*. Berlin: Gestalten, 2013.

Bell, Michael. *Slow Space*. New York: the Monacelli Press, 1998.

Neil Denari:

Denari, Neil. *Interrupted Projections*. Tokyo: TOTO publication, 1996.

Denari, Neil. *Gyropscopic Horizons*. New York: Princeton Architectural Press, 1999.

Denari, Neil. *MassX; Precise Form for an Imprecise World. Selected Things, 2000–2017*. AADCU, 2018.

Hernán Díaz Alonso:

Díaz Alonso, Hernán, The Surreal Visions of Hernán Díaz Alonso. London: Thames & Hudson, 2020.

Díaz Alonso, Hernán, *Xefirotarch*. Huazhong University of Science and Technology Press, 2008.

Toyo Ito:

Buntrock, Dana. *Toyo Ito*. London: Phaidon, 2014.

Ito, Toyo. *Architecture, Possible Here? Home-for-All*. Tokyo, 2013.

Ito, Toyo. *Architecture Words 8: Tarzans in the Media Forest*. London: Architectural Association, 2011.

Kengo Kuma:

Kuma, Kengo. *Architecture Words 2: Anti-Object*. London: Architectural Association, 2013.

Kuma, Kengo. "Kengo Kuma: Digital Gardening." *Space Design*. Tokyo: Kajima Publishing, 1997.

Kuma, Kengo. *Kengo Kuma: Complete Works*. London: Thames & Hudson, 2018.

Paul Lewis:

Lewis, Paul, Marc Tsurumaki, and David Lewis. *Lewis.Tsurumaki.Lewis: Opportunistic Architecture*. New York: Princeton Architectural Press, 2007.

Evans, Robin. *The Projective Cast: Architecture and Its Three Geometries*. Cambridge: the MIT Press, 1995.

Takashi Murakami:

Murakami, Takashi. *Superflat*. Tokyo: MADRA Publishing Co. Ltd., 2001.

O'Doherty, Brian. *Against the White Cube: The Ideology of the Gallery Space*. Santa Monica: the Lapis Press, 1976.

Murakami. Takashi. *Summon Monsters? Open The Door? Heal? Or Die?* Tokyo: Hiropon Factory, 2005.

Albert Pope:

Corner, James. *Taking Measures Across the American Landscape*. New Haven: Yale University Press, 1996.

Pope, Albert. *Ladders*. 2nd ed. New York: Princeton Architectural Press, 2015.

Wolf D. Prix:

Kramer, Thomas. *Prinz Eisenbeton 6: Rock over Barock: Young and Beautiful: 7+2*. Vienna: Springer: 2007.

Noever, Peter (ed.), *In the Absense of Raimund Abraham: Vienna Architecture Conference 2010*. Berlin: Hatje Cantz, 2011.

Prix, Wolf D. *Wolf D. Prix & Coop Himmelb(l)au: Get Off My Cloud: Texts 1968–2005*. Berlin: Hatje Cantz, 2006.

Ali Rahim:

Rahim, Ali. *Catalytic Formations: Architecture and Digital Design*. Abingdon-on-Thames: Taylor & Francis Group, 2006.

Rahim, Ali. *Contemporary Techniques in Architecture*. Academy Press, 2002.

Rahim, Ali. *Contemporary Processes in Architecture*. Academy Press, 2000.

Rahim, Ali and Hina Jamelle, ed. "Elegance," *Architectural Design*, 2007.

Thompson, D'Arcy Wentworth. *On Growth and Form*, 1917.

Lynn, Greg. *Animate Form*. New York: Princeton Architectural Press, 2011.

Hani Rashid:

Rashid, Hani and Lise Anne Couture. *Asymptote Architecture: Actualizations*. Beijing: AADCU, 2010.

Rashid, Hani and Lise Anne Couture. *Flux*. London: Phaidon Press, 2002.

Rashid, Hani and Lise Anne Couture. *SCAPE – Asymptote Architecture*. Seoul: Damdi, 2004.

Rashid, Hani and Lise Anne Couture. *Architecture At The Interval*. New York: Rizzoli International Publications, 1995.

DeLeuze, Gilles and Felix Guattari. *A Thousand Plateaus: Capitalism and Schizophrenia*. Minneapolis: University of Minnesota Press, 1987.

Jesse Reiser:

Reiser, Jesse. *Atlas of Novel Tectonics*. New York: Princeton Architectural Press, 2006.

Reiser + Umemoto. *0-14: Projection and Reception*. London: AA Publications, 2012.

Reiser + Umemoto. *Projects and Their Consequences*. New York: Princeton Architectural Press, 2019.

Jonathan Solomon:

Solomon, Jonathan, Adam Frampton, and Clara Wong. *Cities Without Ground: A Hong Kong Guidebook*. San Francisco: ORO Editions, 2012.

Sant'Elia, Antonio. *La Citta Nuova*, 1914.

Sanford Kwinter, "La Citta Nuova: Modernity & Continuity," in *Zone 1/2*, New York: 1986, p.88–89.

Banham, Reyner. *Megastructure: Urban Futures of the Recent Past*. London: Thames & Hudson, 1981.

Michael Speaks:

Speaks, Michael. "Design Intelligence," *A+U*, December 2002.

Jameson, Fredric. *Postmodernism, or, The Cultural Logic of Late Capitalism*, Durham: Duke University Press, 1991.

■ RELATED TEXTS

Sarah Whiting:

Assemblage

POINT: Essays on Architecture

Whiting, Sarah. "Superblockism: Chicago's Elastic Grid," *Histories of Cities: Design and Context*, eds. Rodolphe el-Khoury and Edward Robbins. London: Spon/Routledge, 2004, p.57–76.

Michael Young:

Young, Michael and John Heskett. *Works in China*, 2011.

OBSERVATIONS: A PLATFORM

BY
WEIJEN WANG

Professor
Department of Architecture at the University of Hong Kong

Facing global challenges on ecology, technology, cultural, and social conflicts, can architecture re-position itself to address these challenges through re-framing its discourse? How can architectural education enable future architects to advance its disciplinary knowledge while taking progressive positions in the production of architecture for the betterment of the human condition and the environment?

We consider the public lecture series at HKU Architecture a classroom for students of all years and programs, a platform for the school and professional communities to exchange ideas and shape collective concerns.

Between 2011 and 2016, the lecture series identified clear themes for each semester: On_Speed, In_Form, Project_ing; local/locus, tectonic/technology, sustain/support; social/capital, culture/artifacts, audiences, reflecting various critical issues in architecture.

David Erdman took the task of coordinating the public lecture series in 2011. As the head of the Department of Architecture, I worked with David on this series in 2012 and 2013, and continued working with other colleagues on the series until 2016. With immense commitment and dedication, David demonstrated great capacity in bringing in a variety of speakers to share their insights of and reflections on issues of our concern. David carefully crafted his introductions before each talk like a prologue before an essay.

These introductory articles reflect not only the way he perceives the work of these speakers, but also the way he frames issues of architecture. This book and each article compiled within its pages are valuable records of our efforts in shaping the platform for architecture at this place in time.

IMAGE CREDITS

IMAGE CREDITS ■

200

■ IMAGE CREDITS

ACKNOWLEDGMENTS

Nearly eight years after these events occurred, I am drafting these acknowledgments. It is weird, to say the least. A pandemic and social unrest have marked Hong Kong and New York City where I now reside. I am a father and (in the role I assumed in 2016 at Pratt Institute as the chairperson of Graduate Architecture) I find myself writing these words enmeshed in the throes of what all of these shifts and changes promise; as well as the challenges they present to our discourse, profession, and education.

In reflection, it is humbling to have been given the privilege and responsibility to curate and organize these events and introductions in a foreign country, one caught between colonialism and post-colonialism, on the edge of sub-tropical climatological change, and to be endowed with the trust of my colleagues to test and experiment with this platform. The material is not obvious, nor intended to be easily consumable. It is intended (as Cole Roskam points out in his Foreword, page 4) to invert assumptions about obvious matters. To stare down what was directly facing us as a faculty and school and (within a sociopolitical and environmental constellation of climates I am witnessing from New York City today) to test the waters in unexpectedly sage and prescient matters.

It is with all of these overlapping histories and their complexities, within the ecologies of today's discussions and discourse, that I want to first and foremost thank all of the participants, many of whom are close friends and others of whom were new acquaintances, for their willingness to address the subjects and (in many cases) engage in extended dialogue about their presentation and the introduction. Equally important are all of the members of the HKU and Hong Kong design community, students and faculty, who attended these events and diligently supported these efforts. Prior to thanking some of them in name, I must also first (and foremost) thank my loving wife Karvina and my son Owen for granting me many late night and early morning "hall passes" to focus on this project—between significant changes in life style, civic style, and career.

Many colleagues prodded and encouraged the preceding pages. Dean Chris Webster and (former) heads of the DoA Jonathan Solomon (followed by) Weijen Wang, daringly cleared and sustained the space for this platform (as Wang has described it in his "Observations") to develop it, allow it to take shape and to witness its transformation. Mind you this was done just prior to the "Umbrella Revolution" and involved the social politics of the moment leading up to 2014, and which contained the threads of recent (significantly more contentious) struggles between domestic and international liberties and inequities in Hong Kong and the global stage; shaping the configuration of speakers and discussions surrounding the value of their contributions.

Many faculty were privy to ill formed and improvised conversations and thinking around these growing, complex issues, providing patient feedback, insight, and pointing out my naive assumptions; as a foreigner and as someone keen to learn. Among them Joshua Bolchover, Jason Carlow, Kristof Crolla, Natalia Echeverri, John Lin, Cole Roskam, Eric Schuldenfrei (now head), Dorothy Tang, Thomas Tsang, Ivan Valin, Tom Verebes, Koon Wee, and Eunice Wong, among others. My former business partner Clover Lee was an invaluable resource of continuous feedback and support throughout these efforts and during a time in which our collaborative practice (davidclovers 2007–2016; recapitulated as plusClover) saw intense growth and development.

Finally, to my patient colleagues at ORO including Gordon Goff and Jake Anderson, Julia van den Hout of Original Copy, the editor, and the design assistants who laid out initial drafts of the book (Joonmo Ai and Kammy Leung), the commitment and acumen you (and others within your organizations) brought to this project was astounding and above the call of duty.

Thank you all once again for your encouragement. This would not have happened without you.